2-26-65

DATE DUE

I^d OCT 19 2001	

THE TEACH YOURSELF BOOKS
EDITED BY LEONARD CUTTS

THE ORGAN

**Uniform with this volume
and in the same
series**

TEACH YOURSELF
TO COMPOSE MUSIC

TEACH YOURSELF
HISTORY OF MUSIC

TEACH YOURSELF
JAZZ

TEACH YOURSELF
MUSIC

TEACH YOURSELF
ORCHESTRATION

TEACH YOURSELF
TO PLAY THE PIANO

TEACH YOURSELF
TO SING

TEACH YOURSELF
SONGWRITING

Photograph by courtesy of the John Compton Organ Co. Ltd.

Organ in the church of St. Michael and All Angels, Bournemouth

TEACH YOURSELF

THE ORGAN

FRANCIS ROUTH
M.A., F.R.C.O., L.R.A.M.
*Organist, St. Philip's Church,
Kensington, London, W.8.*

THE ENGLISH UNIVERSITIES PRESS LTD
102 NEWGATE STREET
LONDON, E.C.1

In memory of
A. WESLEY ROBERTS

First printed 1958
This impression 1963

*Made and Printed in Great Britain for the English Universities Press, Ltd., London
by C. Tinling & Co., Ltd., Liverpool, London and Prescot.*

PREFACE

THE organ has rightly been described as the "King of Instruments"; its past history is a long one, its sound is majestic. Yet you may feel rather apprehensive as you sit at the console and view the formidable array of stops, keys, buttons and pedals that confront you to right and left. And since every organ is different in some way from every other one, my job in this book is as problematic as yours!

But let me sound a word of encouragement. If you can play the piano you have already made a considerable start. Of course the "touch" of a piano and an organ are quite different, but if your fingers are used to the keyboard and have been trained to "work", then you will soon adapt them to their new surroundings. You will at once enjoy discovering the wealth of tone-colour that the organ contains. A knowledge of musical rudiments, notation, simple terms and so on, is necessary for any aspiring organist. Those who wish to make sure of these are advised to refer to the companion volumes on music in this series: *Teach Yourself Music* and *Teach Yourself to Play the Piano*.

Most vicars and organists will have no objection to your practising on their organ—so long as you ask their permission at the beginning and remember to turn off the wind and the lights when you have finished! If you live in London it is possible to practise on the organ at the Royal College of Organists, Kensington Gore. In every case there will probably be a nominal charge to cover the cost of electricity used. It is also possible to practise at home by having a pedal attachment fitted to the piano. Likewise a harmonium will acquaint you with the sound and the "feel" of a wind instrument not unlike an organ.

Each chapter in the book deals with one aspect of organ playing, and contains exercises to illustrate the various

points raised. The best approach would be to acquire the
pieces from which the examples are taken, and apply the
lessons learnt from the exercises to the remainder of the
pieces. Chapters I to VIII deal with the basic knowledge
and technique required by the organist in order to lay sure
foundations for his playing. Chapters IX to XIII deal with
broader musical problems which have to be solved with
particular reference to the organ—Registration, Rhythm and
Phrasing (so often ignored by organists), choosing works
to play, organ accompaniment, and finally the different
types of organ, particularly the cinema organ. Chapter XIV
is devoted to general musicianship.

For those whom the book excites to proceed further (and
I can assure them that the field is large, particularly where
organ building is concerned), there is a short bibliography
at the end.

CONTENTS

THE ORGAN

CHAPTER I

INTRODUCING THE ORGAN

Chief characteristics — Stops — Manuals — Pedals
— Connection with the Church

IMAGINE yourself as a listener in a cathedral or large church while the organ is being played. The sound will probably come from above the place where you are, giving the impression of filling the whole building with a rich, resounding tone. There are few people who have not had this experience, for example at the end of a Service; but exactly the effect it produces is difficult to analyse in words and everyone would, if asked, give a different description.

Played loudly, the organ can produce an effect of majestic dignity, solemn or ceremonious, sad or joyful, aptly rounding off the Service. Played quietly, it can distil an atmosphere of calm, reverence, mystery, distance, as nothing else. No other instrument can equal the organ in sustaining a passage of extreme quietness.

What are the ingredients which go to make up the whole effect? First there is the resonance natural to a large building. Every sound lingers in the air, as it were, and the louder chords give the impression of floating upwards before they die away. Each sound tends to merge into the one just before it, producing a continuous tone. Then, of course, there is the variety of sounds. The different types of stops and their characteristics will be discussed in more detail in the next chapter, but you should be aware from the start that there is an enormous range and variety of sound-colours at the organist's disposal, from the thickest and heaviest to the lightest and quietest—even on a small-sized organ.

You might have noticed that the organist is **able** to sustain a note or a chord, or to keep the same level and quality of tone over a passage of music for just as long as he wishes. A snare indeed! To put it crudely, a note will remain sounding as long as it remains pressed down, and quite ˙obviously if certain stops are in use, (or "drawn"), they will remain operative unless the organist does something about them! This may seem elementary, but it has far-reaching implications in organ playing which will, I hope, become apparent later.

Conversely, and just as important, the organist is able to switch at a moment's notice from playing loudly to playing quietly, or of course to any intermediate volume; or from playing loudly with one quality of tone to playing loudly with another. Particularly if you listen to a piece of any length you will probably hear a passage of contrasting volume and tone-quality introduced at some point. This brings you to consider the different keyboards (or manuals) of the organ, each of which has its own characteristic stops.[1] The smallest organ would be content with one manual, a number have two; most parish church organs have three; cathedral organs, as you would expect, have four, and sometimes five.

Next, as you listen, you might notice that the Bass line is independent. Played with the feet on separate pedals, the bass part provides the underlying foundation of the whole musical structure. But just as the 'cellos and basses in an orchestra would not necessarily play continuously in a piece of any length, so the pedals in an organ piece might well have one or more periods of silence before coming in again. Very impressive it can be if the organist builds up a substantial volume of tone with manuals alone—and yet you are aware that something is missing—then the pedals are introduced, instantly making the musical structure complete. (This is called a "Pedal Entry".) The Pedals

---

[1] The manuals will be discussed in detail in Chapter III.

(or "pedal organ") have their own independent and individual stops.[1]

Lastly, it is important to realize the inevitable connection between the organ and the Church. It is a connection which has its roots in history. By far the majority of organs are situated in a church; you are probably anxious to "teach yourself" the organ through being in some way connected with your local church. And although there are organs in other buildings, (for example town halls, and the Royal Festival Hall and the Royal Albert Hall in London, and many cinemas) it is in church that the organ "sounds right"—though possibly only because that is what we have always known. The importance of this organ — church connection, and its bearing on organ playing, and organ music, will be seen later. At this moment, as you simply listen and realise the effect and beauty of the organ properly played in a cathedral or large church, ask yourself whether the effect would be the same in the "cold blood" of the concert hall—even with the same organist, and the same piece of music!

From this you will see that by aspiring to play the organ you put yourself in direct line with the mainstream of European music from a long way back in the past. Your field of practical study covers the stops, their variety and type as well as their use, the manuals, the pedals (each with their own problems), the technique of combining these different elements, points of performance which are peculiar to the organ—particularly the resonance of the building in which you play—and last, but by no means least, the literature for the organ.

Now let us examine point by point the various stages along the way.

[1] The pedals need not play the bass part, though they usually do, (cf. Chapter VIII), and of course a Pedal Entry can occur in any passage, not necessarily a loud one. The above is only one example.

CHAPTER II

THE STOPS

*How stops are named — Mutations and Mixtures — Flues and
Reeds — Diapasons, flutes, strings — Types of reed stops — Extra
stops — Couplers — Draw-stops, tabs — Combination pistons*

PERHAPS it should be made clear before we embark on a
more detailed study of the various aspects of organ-playing
that this is not intended to be a detailed technical treatise.
Books of a technical nature are listed in the bibliography at
the end of the book. To understand an organ fully from the
mechanical and electrical points of view would obviously
be a formidable task, and in any case not necessarily
relevant to the business of playing. So I propose to leave
aside all technical points except those which are of direct
importance to the player.

To start with, we can take it as known that when you
switch on the current you are completing an electrical
current by means of which air is circulated through the
bellows. Without this the organ would make no sound at
all. Exactly how this is achieved, and to what wind-pressure,
is beyond the scope of this book. An even, steady wind-
pressure is of the greatest importance in achieving a good
tonal result; but this is the concern of the builder and the
designer. You as the organist have to play the instrument
as it is! It might however be of interest to note that there are
still a few small organs in existence, particularly in country
churches, whose bellows are worked by hand.

If there is any mechanical or electrical defect, or any stop
particularly out of tune, it is always better to call in the
organ builders. Tuning is a delicate and complicated
business, and unskilled tampering may well do serious

damage. Even apparently simple repairs had far better be
left to the trained expert.

Generally speaking, each stop possesses a rank, or row, of
pipes, one pipe for each note of the manual; and underneath the names of the different stops you will see a number
(e.g. 4, 8, 16, etc.). These numbers refer to the length in
feet of the lowest in that particular rank of pipes, and
determine the pitch of the stop. An 8′ stop will sound at the
pitch corresponding to the note pressed; a 16′ stop will
sound an octave lower; a 4′ stop an octave higher; a 2′ stop
two octaves (i.e. a fifteenth) higher. There are also stops
called "mutation" stops[1] which sound at various pitches
intermediate to these octave divisions; and "mixture"
stops which, as the name implies, sound at a number of
pitches different from that of the note pressed. A mixture
stop has one rank of pipes for each interval that it sounds.[2]

Thus if you draw an 8′ stop and play middle C, middle C
will sound; with a 16′ stop drawn, the C below middle C
will sound; with a 4′ stop drawn, the C above middle C
will sound; with a 2′ stop drawn, the C two octaves above
middle C will sound.

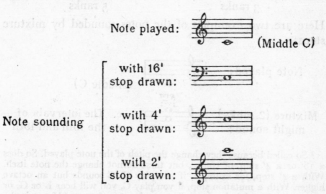

From now on we shall refer to stops as being 8′, 16′, etc.

See next page for footnotes.

Mutation Stops

The name of a mutation stop will usually indicate what interval there is between the note which sounds and the note you play. For example:

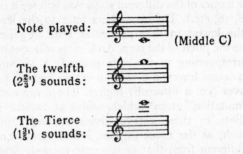

Note played: (Middle C)

The twelfth
($2\frac{2}{3}'$) sounds:

The Tierce
($1\frac{3}{5}'$) sounds:

Mixture Stops

These stops have several ranks of pipes, one for each note sounding, and usually the name of the stop will indicate how many ranks it possesses, e.g.:

Mixture   Mixture
3 ranks   5 ranks

Here are two examples of the notes sounded by mixture stops:—

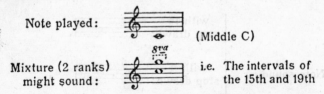

Note played: (Middle C)

Mixture (2 ranks)   i.e. The intervals of
might sound: the 15th and 19th

---

[1] So called because they change the pitch of the note played. So does a 16' or a 4' stop, of course, but these do not change the note itself. With a 4' stop, for example, if you play C, C sounds but an octave higher. With a mutation stop, if you play C, you will hear E or G, or whatever interval it is, depending on the stop drawn. (*Mutare* is the Latin for to change.)

[2] See Appendix 5 for more information about this stop. It is recommended that you leave it over until the end.

Mixture 5 ranks
might sound:

i.e. The intervals of
the 8th (octave),
12th, 15th, 19th, 22nd

Mutation and Mixture stops should, of course, not be used by themselves, but only in combination with other stops to add brightness and brilliance.

Now for the main families. A pipe can either consist of a length of wood or metal with a mouthpiece through which the air is allowed to pass (when you press a particular key) —or the mouthpiece may have a tongue which vibrates (as in the case of the clarinet in an orchestra). The first type of pipes are called "Flues", the second type are called "Reeds". Stops of both categories are found on each manual, and of course on the "Pedal Organ" (as the Pedals should be called).

(a) Flue Stops

First and foremost comes the Diapason,[1] the fundamental tone of the organ. If the top of the pipe is left open, it is called an "Open Diapason"; if it is covered over, it is called a "Stopped Diapason". The latter gives a softer rather more woolly tone. The Open Diapason and Stopped Diapason are usually 8' stops. In the same family are the Double Diapason (16'), Principal (4'), Fifteenth (2').

On some organs you may find more than one Open Diapason on the same manual, e.g. Open Diapason (i), Open Diapason (ii), etc. (The Royal Albert Hall organ has no less than five on one manual!) This simply means that they are graded in power, diameter of pipe etc., the first one naturally being the strongest.

Dulciana (8'), Salicional (8'), Vox Angelica (8'), Salicet (4'), are smaller, gentler versions of the Open Diapason.

So for a solid, dignified quality of tone, two or three

[1] The Greek derivation means simply "through all", i.e. it is the stop common to all manuals, and organs.

manual stops will be found to be sufficient, viz. Open
Diapason, Principal, Fifteenth, (cf. Exercises 13 and 14
below: Also Chapter IX).

Mutation stops (of one rank) and Mixture stops (of more
than one rank) are also of Diapason quality, though their
extremely high pitch might not suggest it. The latter are
given colourful names, e.g. Furniture, Cymbal, Cornet,
Sesquialtera. When the Open Diapason is in use, it is of no
consequence to draw the Stopped Diapason; the latter will
be blanketed—particularly if the Principal (4') is also in
use. The Stopped Diapason, with its quieter tone, really
belongs to the "Flute" group of stops,[1] which we will now
consider.

Stops of the Flute family sound extremely well when
played by themselves or with each other, particularly when
their tone is unspoiled by anything heavier.[2] With the
exception of the Stopped Diapason just mentioned, and
some others, the word "flute" (or German "*flöte*") usually
appears on the stop; and as every organ will have a different
selection of flute stops, it is difficult to make a comprehensive list. But the commonest are:

  Hohlflöte (8'), Claribel (8'), Rohr Flute (8'), Gedact (8'),
  Harmonic Flute (4'), Suabe Flute (4'), Waldflöte (4'),
  Gemshorn (4'), Piccolo (2'), Flautina (2').

Flue stops which, strictly speaking, come neither under
the heading of Diapasons or Flutes, are usually referred to
as "Strings". It is obvious that the organ, being wind-
operated, cannot possibly reproduce accurately the sound of
violins; nevertheless the tone produced by certain stops
does possess a degree of "stringyness"—hence the description. The chief stops under this heading are:

  Gamba, Celeste, Violone, Violin Diapason, Geigen.
They are all usually 8' stops.

The stops which you find on the "Pedal Organ" you
would naturally expect to be largely 16', giving a depth to

---

[1] See Exercise 11.   [2] cf. Chapter IX.

correspond with the 'cellos and basses in an orchestra. Among others, there will probably be: Open Diapason (16'); Violone (16'); Bourdon (16')—the latter being really a stopped Diapason.

(b) Reed Stops

Every organ has its own characteristic reed stops, and one of the first things that strikes a listener about the style of an organist's playing is his use of reeds. The chapter on "Registration"[1] will deal with this in more detail, but suffice it at this point to say that reed tone adds colour and brilliance to the general effect, it is certainly not fundamental. The fundamental tone of the organ is the Diapason.

Reeds vary very much in their power, ranging from the light-voiced oboe or clarinet, to the heavy, almost over-whelming pedal reeds that are found on some organs, and which call for most careful use. The brightness and sharpness of the tone of a reed stop can be affected by the thickness of the tongue, and the shape. Normally reeds of 16' pitch are not so bright as reeds of a higher pitch, though their volume may well be excessive. A quiet pedal reed is in fact a rarity on most English organs.

Starting from the bottom and working upwards the heaviest reeds are Ophicleide (16'); Bombarde (16'); Posaune or Trombone (16'), Fagotto or Bassoon (16'). Manual reeds might include: Tuba (8' or 16'), Trumpet (8' or 16'), Clarion (4' or 8'). Among the quieter reeds are Cornopean (8'), Oboe (8'), Basset Horn (8'), Vox Humana (8'). Thus you will see that stops are described by two factors—their size (i.e. pitch), and their family. So you refer to a "16' reed", "a 4' Flute", etc. etc.

(c) Extra Stops, Couplers

In addition to the main groups of stops so far listed, you will probably find one or two extra ones—notably the Octave

Chapter IX.

and Sub-octave couplers. Their contribution is self-evident. Exactly what these do will be discussed in the next chapter, but they are mentioned here so as to complete our survey of the knobs which face you to right and left as you sit at the manuals (or "console").

All the above mentioned stops are called "speaking" stops since, when they are in use, you can, by pressing the key, make that particular stop "speak".[1] There remain to be mentioned several devices which look like stops but are used for combining various sounds. They are called "couplers", and in most organs of conventional design are placed below the speaking stops, e.g. Swell to Great; Great to Pedal, etc.

If you have on your organ a tremulant, you would be best advised to leave well alone, and only to use it with extreme caution. Normally it is superfluous.

Most pre-war organs have the conventional draw-stops, which the player simply pulls out (towards him) as required. Its name and size are written on the rounded end of the knob. In older organs, to pull out a stop required considerable physical effort; in pictures of them you may have seen the large, unwieldy knobs, in some cases above the player's head; but in modern organs a stop, when drawn, only moves a matter of an inch or two.

A number of organs nowadays do away with the conventional draw-stops and substitute "tabs" or "stop-keys", which are simply pressed down. This movement is considerably easier to carry out than it is to pull out a stop, also the player can see the names on the tabs with greater ease than names on stop-knobs—though some modern organs have a "curved jamb", which means that the draw-stop curves inwards, and so allows the player to see the name with less effort than when it faces directly to the front, as in the case with most organs. Tabs, all of course named, are either arranged in front of the player, or else on either side of him, as is the case with draw-stops.

[1] Organ-builders refer to "voicing" a pipe.

As the organ becomes more complicated and requires more stops, so it becomes increasingly more difficult to manage. To meet this difficulty the modern electro-pneumatic organ[1] has pistons situated under each manual, which when pressed will automatically bring into use certain combinations of stops on that manual; they are therefore called "combination pistons". The same combinations of stops can be obtained by pressing foot-buttons, situated just above the pedals, and numbered to correspond with the finger-operated pistons. On older organs there are only foot pistons (or levers) to be found, though they often work by a direct leverage, in which case they need to be treated with caution as the stops they are supposed to operate may not be fully drawn out. If you find this to be the case with your organ, it is best not to use them but to draw all stops by hand.

The "Double Touch Canceller" is a device needing special mention. It is only found on some instruments, and is a convenient way of reducing the stops in use down to one, particularly if you are using a fairly heavy combination, and to reduce them by the usual means would be inconvenient. But do not rely on this method, certainly at first.

In organists' jargon, Swell 3 (for example) is a convenient way of describing that particular combination of stops obtained by pressing the third combination piston on the Swell Manual—hand or foot, it makes no difference.

Finally a word of caution about the combination pistons. Do not accept them as final! They were probably set by the builders, or by your predecessor, and certainly do not represent the law of the Medes and Persians. Later on, when you have mastered the different types of stops, you will be perfectly justified in making your own combinations. And even then, do not play exclusively according to your re-arranged sets. You should be constantly trying out fresh

[1] See Chapter III.

ideas. Even with a small organ, it is remarkable how many different combinations of sound you can produce.

First refer to the beginning of the next chapter. (If yours is an older type organ, without combination pistons, then go straight to Exercise 7.)

(1) Without drawing any stops, play this chord of C on the Swell with the right hand (R.H.).

With the left hand (L.H.) press the 1st button on the left under the Swell Manual.[1] Hold the chord for a few moments, really listening to the sound.

(2) Without raising the R.H. at all, press the next combination piston with the L.H., listening carefully.

(3) Continue to press one piston after another, listening carefully. You will notice that the tone becomes progressively fuller and richer as you go on, until the last ("Full Swell") is reached.

(4) Now repeat this, but using foot pistons, and raising R.H. between each combination of stops.

(5) Repeat this exercise on the Great.

(6) Repeat this exercise on the Choir. In this case you will notice a difference, namely that most of the pistons do not give you a progressive increase of tone, but only different solo stops—one of which may be a powerful reed!

All these exercises are of course only for the manual stops. Next you should discover for yourself the full tonal resources you have available on your organ.

[1] This may turn out to be a "coupler". (See page 28.) If so, then go on to the next one.

SWELL

(7) Without drawing any stops, play this chord of C on the Swell with the R.H.

Look among the Swell stops, and find all those of the Flute family. Draw them one after the other, starting with 8', then adding 4' and 2'.

(8) Pushing in the flute stops, now investigate the String toned stops (still holding the same chord); you should find one or two.

(9) Pushing in the String-toned stops, now start on those of Diapason quality. Begin with those of 8' (or 16' if there is one) and work up to 4' and 2'. Now, without lifting the R.H., add any 8' reed stops there may be (oboe, cornopean, etc.); next the 4' reeds (clarion, etc.); next the 16' reed, if there is one. Next any mutation stops.

(10) Now lift your R.H. There should be only one type of stop remaining which you have not tried out—the mixture. So draw any mixture stops and play the chord of C again. There, once more, you will have the "Full Swell", though perhaps not with quite the same combination of stops as you got from pressing the last combination piston (Ex. 3 and 4). As an experiment, add stops of "flute" quality and see if there is any noticeable difference to the volume. Of course there will not be! Now press the last piston on the right (under the Swell manual) and see what combination of stops it gives you. Compare this with your last combination. If there is an Octave and Sub-octave coupler add them one after the other, listening for the result.

GREAT

(11) Push in all the stops used in Ex. 10. Without drawing any stops, play the chord of C on the Great. Pick out the Flute stops, and draw them one by one; 8' first, then 4',

then 2'. (Remember that the Stopped Diapason counts as a Flute stop.)

(12) Pushing in the Flute stops, repeat this with the String-toned stops.

(13) Pushing in the String-toned stops, and without playing, draw Open Diapason (8'), Principal (4'). Play the chord of C.

(14) Without lifting R.H. add the Fifteenth (2'), and any more Diapason tone stops there are, up to mutations and mixtures. You will now get a solid block of tone—so be careful not to hold the chord for too long!

(15) Pushing in all the Diapason stops used in Ex. 14, play a note or scale (preferably not a chord), while drawing one by one the Reeds. (Be prepared for a heavy sound.) It is better to try them individually, pushing in one, before drawing the next. But if your organ has reeds of 16', 8' and 4' try them together, playing the chord of C.

(16) Push in the Reeds, and with the chord of C press the combination pistons again, one after the other starting from the left,[1] and compare the gradual increase you get from them with what you have been playing in Ex. 14. Notice particularly what stops are in use with particular combinations.

CHOIR

(17) Push in all the stops used in Ex. 16. Playing the chord of C on the Choir, draw all the Flute stops, beginning with 8'.

(18) Push in the Flute stops, and draw the String-toned stops one after the other.

(19) Pushing in the String stops, and playing a single note or scale, draw each of the remaining stops one by one. Decide which category they all belong in. It is on the Choir manual that you will find such colourful solo stops as Orchestral Oboe, Cor Anglais, and other reeds.

[1] Again, the extreme left one may be a coupler.

It should now be apparent that certain stops, particularly reed stops, are more suitable for solo work, while others are of greater effect when added to other stops. The former are called "solo" stops, the latter "chorus" stops.

By this time you should have heard all the stops that are available on your organ (with the exception of the Pedal Stops). How they can best be used is one of the organist's main problems. The first essential step is to understand them, and to hear them both individually and together.

CHAPTER III

THE MANUALS

Characteristic difference between the various manuals — Couplers — Tracker action — Electro-pneumatic action — Touch — Manual technique — Detached console

THE frontispiece shows the layout of a typical 3-manual organ; such an organ as you would expect to find in an average-sized Parish Church. The lowest manual nearest the player is called the Choir; next the Great; the highest of the three is called the Swell. If your instrument has two manuals, the lowest is the Great, above it the Swell. It is important to know the corresponding French and German names for the manuals, as indeed for other parts of the instrument since when we discuss music to play (Chapter XI) you will find a large proportion of French and German composers' music is recommended. The commonest terms that you will need are listed in the Glossary.

The compass of the Manuals is five octaves—61 notes. That is to say from the C two octaves below middle C, to the C three octaves above it. This is the same for all manuals. The lowest note on the pedals is the same (low C) as the lowest note on the manuals.

How to differentiate between one manual and another; how to decide which to use at any particular moment; these points must first be settled.

The chief manual is the Great, on which you will find the basic stops of the instrument—particularly of course Diapasons, of various sizes and descriptions. The larger your organ, the more mutations and mixtures you will find on the Great Organ, the more impressive your tonal build-up will be. Yet you can build up an effective "Flue chorus" with 3 or 4 stops. If you see written in the score "Great to Fifteenth" that means that the Great is built up with sufficient weight for the Fifteenth not to sound too much; in other words a fairly solid body of Diapason tone, with the Fifteenth added for brilliance.

You will probably have one or more Reed stops on the Great, which may well be loud and heavy—only suitable for passages of a climactic nature (Exercise 15, Chapter II).

So you can easily see that the Great manual (or Great Organ as it should really be called, as each manual and the pedals is a complete "organ" in itself) is the most important, and the loudest; but not necessarily the most colourful.

The manual above it, the Swell, contains the quietest stops on the organ. Moreover, on the Swell you will find Chorus Reeds (see page 25) which are more amenable to the ear and less overwhelming than the Reed(s) found on the Great. The former used with mixtures and mutations, and with or without a diapason (to give "body") give the characteristic "Full Swell". It is very important to understand that the term "Full Swell" is a description of tone rather than volume. Although it adds fulness and brilliance when superimposed on an already existing f and can be distinctly heard above it, nevertheless it is perfectly possible to introduce it by itself, with the Swell Box shut (see Chapter V) in a passage marked p.

In order to hear the difference between the Swell and the Great, try out and compare stops of the same description (e.g. Open Diapason) on each manual. You will see that an Open Diapason on the Swell is nothing like so large and imposing as an Open Diapason on the Great. Next, as I have already mentioned, the Swell has a wide selection of quiet stops—a great snare for the sentimental or the un-rhythmical player, but just as much a great potential source of beauty. They will give you almost endless pleasure to discover, particularly if you use them singly, and do not cross different tone-qualities. (The Swell Octave is a most useful way of adding 4' tone if you desire it.) May I here enter a plea for the most careful use of that extraordinary pair, the Vox Humana and the Voix Celeste? It has always seemed strange that the curious wobble produced by these two should be thought to resemble either the voice of humans or the voice of angels; in any case, a little goes a long way.

The Choir Organ has been designed by most English builders partly for purposes of accompaniment, partly for special solo effects. Quiet stops of a pure quality are therefore found on it. In addition you will find a selection of solo stops ranging from light-voiced reeds to (perhaps) a powerful Tromba or Tuba.

By means of the non-speaking stops, or Couplers, it is possible to couple two manuals together, and to couple the pedals to any manual as desired. If, for example, you draw Swell to Great, you can play on the Great manual and at the same time make use of any stops that are drawn on the Swell, which will sound as well. Two sets of stops are thus available on the same manual. It is also possible to couple Swell to Choir and Choir to Great.

The pedals can be coupled to any manual. But if you draw Great to Pedal the sound when you play the pedals will be made up of the Pedal stops plus any stops that are drawn on the Great. Some small organs are deficient in pedal stops, perhaps only having one or two 16′ (Big and Little Boom); such a deficiency can often be made up by coupling the pedals to a manual which can provide the missing 8′ or 4′ tone.

If you have been playing on the Great and you then decide to play quietly on the Swell, remember to push in Great to Pedal; otherwise your bass line will dominate proceedings until you realise what is the matter.

So much for the main characteristics of the various manuals. As you will find when we discuss Registration, there is no substitute for your own personal acquaintance with the particular sound produced by a stop. As an example of this, the Oboe stop on your Swell manual may have a smooth, rounded-off quality, while the corresponding Oboe on the organ down the road may be harsh and raucous in the extreme.

What appears the same on paper—or rather on ivory—in respect of its description and size may well not be the same in sound. That is why specifications of organs are not the end of the story; it is always the sound that matters. The specifications I give (page 138) are to show typical distribution of stops in organs of different character, and to show how the tonal build-up is achieved in different ways at different periods.

To return to the manuals, let us quickly consider what happens when the key is pressed down. Old organs, that is to say organs built up till about the middle of the nineteenth century—obviously it is not possible to draw a hard and fast dividing line—have what is called a "tracker" action; modern organs have an electro-pneumatic action. The action by which a note sounds is nothing whatever to do with the tone quality or sound of an organ (in fact old pipes are very often used in restored and new organs on account of their mellowness and excellent quality) but is simply the means whereby that tone is produced.

Tracker action consists of a direct system of levers between the key and the pallet—a lid covering the foot of the pipe. When you press down the manual key you operate levers which in turn open the pipe, which then speaks. As your finger is itself a muscular lever, it is clear that one enormous advantage of this action is that you are in direct touch with the sound you produce, particularly as the whole process is instantaneous. You should really feel that your fingers are directly responsible for the sound, even though (as is sometimes the case) a "double pallet" may give the effect of first pressure and second pressure when you play a note.

The combination pedals on a tracker action organ of course work on the same principle of direct leverage. Therefore the more stops they are supposed to operate the heavier they will be! This is an additional reason for drawing stops when possible by hand.

The modern electro-pneumatic action is much lighter and easier (the key resistance is 3-5 oz.) as well as being more efficient. Its great advantage is that it enables the player to change stops by means of thumb-operated pistons situated under the manuals, as already discussed. But you may find that the action is too easy for your fingers, particularly if you have been used to the old-fashioned heavier action; and smudgy, untidy playing may well result.

Whatever type of instrument you play, whether ancient or modern, the fundamental principle of touch is the same. Crisp, clean, clear finger action is the most vital ingredient of manual technique. This applies just as much to chords as to single notes. If you play a chord of three notes with one hand, your fingers must be so trained that each one of those three notes is played exactly at the same moment. On a modern instrument it requires the merest contact with the key to make a note speak. Also the hand must be raised perfectly evenly at the end of the duration of the chord; no note must be left untidily finished. As hymn tunes consist largely of chords, they provide a good starting point in clean fingering.

It makes absolutely no difference whether a note is played with the utmost gentleness or with the most heavy and savage attack—as seems to have been necessary with the earliest organs, in which the key required the full weight of the fist to press it down. No accentuation is possible this way; the mouth of the pipe is either open or shut, and the speed with which the key is pressed down is of no consequence. It follows therefore that there is no useful purpose to be served by stiffening up the wrist, applying extra weight, or bringing the arm to bear on the key. The wrist must invariably be flexible, especially to avoid muscular tension and stiffness, and the fingers alone move; the shoulders and forearm remain still.

Manual technique consists primarily in clean, active

finger-work; as it is so easy to make a note sound, there must be the most definite division—however short—between one and the next, particularly in a quick moving passage. Just as you "pick up your feet" while walking, so the fingers must never be allowed to drag wearily from one note to the next, with no clear-cut division between.

If you are a pianist—and it is a great advantage if you are—then you will know that when playing the piano it is possible to bring out a particular part by playing it with more weight than the rest, and thus to make a solo of that part. Of course this is impossible on one manual of the organ. Apart from the tune, which sounds above the rest by its being simply the highest part, the only way available to you of bringing out a part as a solo is by playing it on another manual, with a stop which is sufficiently different in character or volume from the remainder for it to be picked out. This, however, does not apply to the cinema organ, when the principle of "double touch" enables the player to bring out a melody on the same manual as its accompaniment. (See Chapter XII.)

So clean finger-work is of the first importance. Arising out of that, one of the very few expressive devices available to the organist is to make a clean break by lifting the hand between one group of notes (or "phrase") and the next. The organ would be only too happy to give you a continuous sound for just as long as you ask it to; but from the point of view of musicianship and interesting playing it is essential to let in the daylight between one block of sound and the next. The most effective way of accenting a note and directing the listener's attention towards it, is quite simply by shortening the previous one, thus letting in the daylight.

So if I wanted to play:—

I could only achieve it by playing:—

or even:—

The amount of pressure I bring to bear on the second, the accented note, or the force with which I play it, are quite irrelevant; it is the rest before it that brings it into prominence. Of course I could always add to the effect by drawing another stop during the period of the rest, but the fundamental principle is one of clean finger-work in manual technique. Nothing is more unmusical than to drift vaguely from one succession of held chords to another, probably over a low sustained pedal note; unfortunately, as I have said, the organ in this respect is only too willing to oblige you, with its sustained tone. This subject will be raised again under the heading of Improvisation (Chapter XIV).

Try the exercises at the end of this chapter mainly with a view to developing an easy-moving, active, and clean finger technique. Then if you take up the pieces from which the exercises are extracts, you can apply the same principles to the rest. Every exercise which I give at the end of different chapters is taken from a piece of music which is included in the suggested list of pieces given at the end of Chapter XI.

It is always advisable to write your own fingering in the copy. It will serve to remind you, when you next look at a piece, of the way you took it last time. This is particularly important if you do not have the opportunity to play the organ as often as you would like. You can in this way both teach yourself and save time.

You should aim to achieve the utmost possible independence between the two hands. It should make no difference to your ease of movement whether you play the Right Hand on the Great, Left Hand on the Swell; or Right Hand on the Swell, Left Hand on the Great; or Right Hand on the Choir, Left Hand on the Swell; or both hands on the same manual—or any other variation. Practise the exercises at the end of this chapter in different ways; also vary the speeds, and introduce different qualities of touch (staccato, legato).

While on the subject of independence, one of the most important aspects of technique which you should try to develop is the ability to begin or finish a phrase in the left hand at a different moment and independently from one in the right; or again to feel the Alto part as being quite distinct and separate from the Treble part, although both may be played with the same hand. This is just the sort of thing you would expect to find in a Fugue. At first, exaggerate the phrase marks in the various parts; the exercises can be played with particular reference to this point. It will be of help if you play them slowly first, and work up the speed as needed later. In the first exercise, notice particularly that the Alto part, at the point marked + has the Fugue subject in the key of C Major (the piece is in the key of D Minor); this should obviously be phrased in the same way as it was when first given out at the beginning—or "Exposition". The various possible ways of phrasing this subject are discussed in Chapter X.

The manuals, stops and pedals taken as a complete unit are called the Console. Often the Console is detached from the rest of the instrument, though obviously in the case of the old Tracker action this is impossible. In cinemas and theatres the Console is not only detached but also movable!

There is a considerable advantage in the detached Console; chiefly that it enables the player to hear objectively exactly the sound he is producing. Often in the conventional design of organ the sound goes out over his head, and he can only deduce, usually wrongly, what volume he is in fact making; or else he can rely on other people's judgment,

B

which is obviously unsatisfactory. But although this problem is solved by detaching the console, another difficulty is thereby introduced. There is bound to be a certain amount of time lost between the moment the key is pressed down and the moment the sound produced reaches your ear. The greater the distance the longer this time will be. So there is a lot to be said both for and against the detached console; you must be the judge. If your organ has a detached console, try getting the chance of playing one which has not, and decide which you prefer.

The Exercises are taken from the following pieces:

(1) Fugue in D minor.
     No. 2 from Eight short preludes and fugues—*Bach*

(2) Psalm Prelude in E flat. (Set 1, No. 2)—*Herbert Howells*

(3) Allegro from Concerto No. 2 in B flat—*Handel*

EXERCISES

Note: How would you achieve the stress on the E♭ in bar 2?

Handel

1) First play on one manual throughout.
2) Then play *mf* on Great, *p* on Swell.
3) Then play Right hand Great, Left hand Swell.

CHAPTER IV

THE PEDALS

Liberty, equality, fraternity — Position — Toe and heel touch — Flexibility — Finding notes — "Back" and "forward" — Poise — some "dos" and "don'ts"

THE independent part played with the feet often causes alarm and despondency to students of the organ. Let me say at once that this is largely psychological; the pedal part appears more difficult than it is. The first goal towards which your study should be directed has already been suggested in the previous chapter, when we were discussing the manuals—namely independence; in this case between the hands and feet. The exercises are all intended to help you achieve this. Later on, whenever you isolate the pedal part of a passage (as you should, of course) and practise that alone, you should immediately play it in conjunction with the hands, first individually then together, aiming all the time to achieve independence.

One way of considering the matter is by the familiar formula "Liberty, Equality, Fraternity".

> Liberty—because you must on no account "drag your toes"; the feet must not be allowed to follow meekly and mildly what the hands, particularly the Left Hand, happen to be doing. They will tend to unless checked. They must be completely emancipated.

> Equality—Because the pedal part is just as important as the rest, if not more so. Try playing a passage without the pedals and notice how incomplete it sounds.

> Fraternity—because all the parts join together in the same piece of music.

POSITION

You should sit at the console exactly in the centre of the stool. Make sure that the stool is at that height which enables you to play the pedals with reasonable ease; without either being doubled up, and your knees awkwardly bent, or having to lurch forward in order to reach them, the stool being too high. When sitting normally, your feet should just be able to slide along the top of the pedals. Most stools can be adjusted, though unfortunately by no means all.

Heavy, thick-soled walking shoes are not particularly advisable; the pedal organ should not be confused with a treadmill. And for ladies, may I advise against high heels? Ordinary medium-sized shoes are the best; many people prefer evening shoes, as the rather thinner soles enable them to feel with the foot more directly.

Most instruments have a concave radiating pedal board, as shown in the frontispiece; some older ones retain the straight design. In either case the layout, with "white" notes and "black" notes is the same as the keyboard. Although the wood used is the same colour for all pedals, I shall refer to "white" and "black" notes—you may have come across some descriptions of pedals which refer to "long" and "short" notes. It makes little difference, except that "long" and "short" might be taken to refer to note values (crotchets, quavers, etc.).

The compass of the pedals is from C (two octaves below middle C) to F (above middle C). Some organs stop at E; others go up to G. Sit at the console and notice for yourself where the pedal notes are situated in relation to the manuals. (Again, sit exactly in the centre.) With a quiet pedal stop drawn, (e.g. Bourdon, or Echo-Bourdon 16', Bass flute 8') play a few notes at random ranging from the lowest to the highest.

It should be obvious that with each foot you have three possible ways of playing a note:

　　(a) With the heel.
　　(b) With the ball of the foot, left side.
　　(c) With the ball of the foot, right side.

The technique of pedalling consists partly in deciding which of these is the most natural to use at any given moment. For example, with the left foot (heel), play low C; follow this with the next note (C♯) using the toe of the left foot. If when playing C♯ you use the left side of the foot, your leg will be stiffer and more contorted than if you use the right side. Similarly, at the other end of the pedal board, if you play E♭–E with the right foot, it is obviously easier to use the left side of the right toe for the E♭ followed by the heel on E.

One of the very few "rules" which can with safety be laid down is that, just as in the case of the hands you must keep a flexible wrist, so in the business of pedalling you must always ensure that your ankle is flexible. (Make sure again that the organ stool is the right height for you.) There must be the minimum amount of leg-movement, particularly of course if you are playing at speed.

Placing the heel (of either foot) on a "white" note, the toe (of the same foot) on the "black" note next to it, a semi-tone up or down, is one of the commonest and most comfortable sequences of pedalling. You would never use the heel on a "black" note; try doing it, and see for yourself!

Consecutive "black" notes, (e.g. F♯–G♯, C♯–D♯) can easily be taken with the same toe, by rotating the foot from one side to the other. Play F♯–G♯, using the right toe (left side) on F♯, and right toe (right side) on G♯; practise achieving an easy movement while observing how the foot rotates. (Check any tendency for the whole leg to rock, as it well may!) Next with the left toe play C♯ (left side) followed by D♯ (right side) and try to obtain the same movement.

Consecutive "white" notes however (e.g. A–B) should be played toe–heel (or heel–toe) if you are using the same foot; or of course, you could use alternate feet.

The fundamental principle of pedalling can best be described by comparing it with a blind man's reading of

Braille; his fingers feel for the dots, and these are immediately translated into the letters of the words. In exactly the same way an organist feels with his feet; he knows the layout of the pedal board and his feet translate the notes into sounds.

Suppose for example you require the C below middle C. Without looking, feel for the nearest "black" note (in this case C♯), and with the right side of your foot (either foot) against that, you know that the note next under it can only be C. Similarly D can be found with the left side of your foot (either foot) feeling against D♯; B can be found with the left side of the foot feeling against B♭.

And so on. Practise feeling for notes on this principle. I do not suggest for a moment that when you come to play a piece of music *every* pedal note is felt for in this way, of course you will not need to. It is invaluable however when feeling for the first note of a phrase or when you have an awkward leap up or down. The alternative is to take a "lucky dip"! There is, of course, no reason why you should not make use of the pedal light, which the makers so thoughtfully provide. But you must not rely on this "look-and-see" method; apart from anything else, you have not time to conduct a search while playing a piece.

So far so good. Now if you play two consecutive "white" notes with alternate feet (either toes or heels, it makes no difference) you will notice that, in order to avoid treading on yourself, one foot must be drawn slightly behind the other. "White" notes can be played either forward or back; if you need to cross over feet in the course of a passage, then either one foot will need to be placed back while the other crosses over, or it will have to be placed forward while the other crosses under.[1]

When you write your pedalling in the copy—this should always be done, by the way—and you find it necessary to cross feet, it is advisable to write in the word "back" or

[1] See Exercise II.

"forward" as required. The eye easily catches sight of a written word while you are playing, and you are thus reminded. Normally when playing you find there are a thousand things to think about, and the pedals are apt to be forgotten.

Signs used are:—Heel = O or U, Toe = V or Λ. Right foot pedalling is written above the note; left foot pedalling underneath the note.

It is extremely important, having decided on a particular pedalling, to stick to it. Naturally this does not mean that it cannot be altered if you later discover a better pedalling for a particular passage; but you must avoid the haphazard approach, which means that you never decide on a pedalling, never write it in the copy, and probably never use the same pedalling twice.

You will find that in good organ music, lengthy scale or arpeggio passages occur only rarely; but if and when they do it is more than ever necessary to decide on your most comfortable pedalling, write it in, and then practise only that one.

As I have already shown, the toe–heel, or heel–toe sequence (with the same foot, of course) is the most common. Notice how often it occurs in the exercises at the end of this chapter. There is no reason why it should be confined to the interval of a semitone; practise playing D–F♯ with the heel–toe (right side), either foot. The only question you need ask yourself is—can you or can't you play it legato? If you cannot, then you must think of another pedalling. Normally, if you can play a group of notes with one foot and obtain a good legato, it is easier than using two feet for it.

Now practise the following and try to achieve a comfortable movement as the foot rotates:

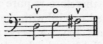

The first toe is obviously left side, the second is right side.
B*

Notes played with the same foot are often bracketed together. Now try this:

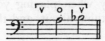

You will notice that in order to play the B♮ it is necessary to slide the heel along the A pedal—very awkward, and most inadvisable! The chances are that it will not be legato. The only answer would be:

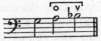

Occasionally, in order to preserve the legato, it is necessary to change feet on a note while keeping it played. See Ex. 3.

Two general points:

(a) Muscular relaxation and ease of movement, particularly at speed, will only be achieved if when playing there is a complete balance and poise between your body, your hands and your feet. It can be shown diagrammatically:

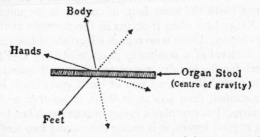

(b) It is important to realise that pedal stops take longer to "speak" than stops of higher pitch. They are more indeterminate, and therefore require more precision when being used. A secure "touch" with the feet is of the greatest importance. Students have a very natural tendency to slither about the pedal board; also of course to play everything with the toe instead of working out a proper pedalling.

Summary of "dos" and "don'ts".

Do: (1) Write in your decided pedalling, at least for the most difficult passages.

(2) Feel for "white" notes by pressing the foot against the adjacent "black" note.

(3) Play as many notes with the same foot as is consistent with legato.

(4) Keep the ankle flexible, the leg still.

(5) Write in the words "forward" or "back" when you need to cross the feet.

(6) Aim for independence.

Don't: (1) Hold up proceedings while you look for the required pedal note.

(2) Take occasional digs in the vague direction of the L.H. end of the pedal board in the hope of providing a "bass-line".

(3) Put your foot on a pedal note and forget about it.

(4) Play the pedal part an octave lower than written (e.g. in a hymn tune). Your 16' pedals already give you an octave below the note played.

(5) Rely on the pedal light.

(6) Play consecutive "white" notes with the same toe.

EXERCISES

(These should be played with quiet pedal stops. Practise slowly first, then at all speeds, ensuring that they are played absolutely in time, legato, and with a flexible ankle.)

The Exercises are taken from the following pieces:

(1) Second movement from Concerto No. 4 in F major
                                        —*Handel*

(2) Rhosymedre—No. 2 from Three Preludes
                                —*Vaughan Williams*

(3) Pastorale.—*Cesar Franck*

(4) Fugue in B flat No. 8 from Eight short preludes and fugues—*Bach*

EXERCISES

CHAPTER V

THE SWELL PEDAL

*General description — Pitfalls to avoid — When and
how the Swell Pedal is used*

THERE are two main types of Swell Pedal that you are
likely to come across. In each case they are situated just in
front of the pedals, thus being accessible to the feet. Far the
commonest nowadays is that type shown in the frontispiece.
The older type, which is now out of date, though you might
find it still, is of this design:—

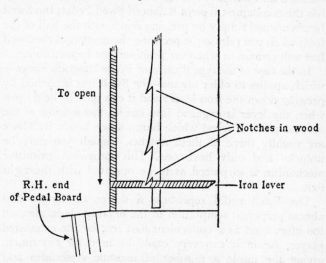

To open

Notches in wood

R.H. end
of Pedal Board

Iron lever

The Swell organ is completely enclosed in a box (called
the Swell box), one side of which consists of wooden shutters,
like a giant Venetian blind. These shutters can be opened

and closed by means of the Swell Pedal, thus producing an effect of "crescendo" or "diminuendo". In some cases these shutters are horizontal, which in the case of early organs means that you can gradually open them, but the moment you release the pressure with your foot they will fall shut again simply by force of gravity, unless checked in some way. The obvious answer to that problem is to have vertical shutters, such as are found on most organs now. These can be left either closed or open, or at any point along the way, by what is called the Balanced Swell.

The Swell is not the only organ that is thus enclosed in a box; the Choir is as well, more often than not. If the organ you play has three manuals, and the Choir organ is "enclosed", there will therefore be two pedals instead of one—one for the Swell box, the other for the Choir box. You can see such an example in the picture. The organ in this case has the commonest type of Balanced Swell Pedal; the Swell box is opened simply by pressing down with the ball of the foot; when you release the pressure, the shutters of the Swell box will remain in whatever position they happen to be.

In the case of the type illustrated in the Diagram above— which applies to older organs—the Swell box is opened by pressing down the iron lever; and it can only be held open when the lever is engaged into one of the notches of the vertical piece of wood which hangs down beside it. There are usually three of these notches, though you may be unlucky and only have one. This somewhat primitive mechanism is so placed as to be operated with the right foot.

The Swell pedal represents a source of danger and almost perpetual temptation to the organist. It is, alas, all too often used as a convenient foot rest for the exhausted player. Again it can very easily be used far too much, giving the music a number of neurotic crescendos and diminuendos and making it move in fits and starts.

The organ lacks expressive devices; the Swell box is one of the very few available. But remember that an organ composer who knows his job will be aware of that, and write music accordingly. This does not of course mean that he writes inexpressive music (which you feel somehow or other it is your bounden duty as the performer to put right) but it does mean that the effect and "expression" of good organ music lies elsewhere, and may not always be apparent at first sight.

THE USE OF THE SWELL PEDAL

The ideal to aim for, though it is a difficult one, is to have such control with the foot that the Swell box is opened (or closed) perfectly evenly and gradually, and with no violent lurches. Not every "hairpin" that you see in the copy means the use of the Swell box by any means. Of course it may mean that; but it may mean an increase of volume by the additon of some stops; or it may simply mean an increase in the general tension of the music, a tightening of the structure; or again (shame to say) it is perfectly possible that it may mean exactly nothing!

The Swell pedal should never be used if by using it the flow of the music in any way suffers—for example, if it detracts your attention from something else of more importance, of if it breaks the pedal legato. This last is a most important point; obviously if both your feet are gainfully employed elsewhere you cannot take one of them away in order to operate the Swell pedal. Normally, of course, when the hands are playing alone a crescendo implies the use of the Swell box.

Strictly speaking, a "hairpin" should begin to operate at that point in the music where it is written, though very often for the reason just given it is necessary to advance or retard the operation of the Swell box.

The Swell pedal is of the greatest assistance, if properly controlled, in sustaining a long held note or chord; it must not be used at all violently, but it can provide just the necessary impulse to give a chord life, particularly if that chord is to be held for any length. And of course, the corollary of that, its controlled use is the most effective way there is of drawing out a diminuendo at the close of a quiet passage. Always remember that the organ can sustain quiet notes for a greater length of time than any other instrument. It can also taper off that note at the close by means of the Swell box.

When you are playing a piece and you open the Swell box slightly you may not detect any difference in volume; perhaps you have not really listened. You therefore proceed to open the box more and more, until before you are aware of it, it is fully open. But I can assure you that the slightest opening or closing can be detected by the listener. For one thing, he may be in a better position to hear than you are (if your organ has not a "detached console"); also his attention is entirely given over to listening, whereas yours is preoccupied with a thousand other things. So get into the habit of really listening, and being content with small movements of the Swell box. There is no need to open (or close) it fully before it makes its effect. Obviously the more stops you have drawn on the Swell, the more true this is. It is particularly true in the case of the "Full Swell".

A final and very important point: when leaving the organ after playing, always leave the Swell and Choir boxes open. This is to ensure the even flow of air through the instrument. If the air in the building becomes either warmer or cooler and the box is shut, the air in the box will be of a different temperature from that elsewhere in the organ when you next come to play, and you may find certain stops out of tune.

EXERCISES

Practise in each example a really gradual, controlled opening and shutting of the Swell box.

(1) Here is an example of a long held note, gradually dying away. Start with the box open, and a quiet selection of stops. The right foot will be needed for the A in the pedal

part in bar 1, although it is marked staccato; the remaining pedal notes can be played with the left foot; so the Swell box can be gradually shut during the last three bars.

(2) Here is an example with hands alone; so the "hairpin" can only be effected with the Swell pedal. Practise a really gradual increase in spite of the rather awkward fingering of bar 3, which needs care to achieve a good legato. Do not forget to couple Swell to Great and draw some Swell stops, otherwise the Swell box will be useless.

(3) And again here. Start with a good rich tone Great; Swell full, with the box completely shut. By gradually opening it, until it is fully open at the *ff*, you can obtain a really dynamic crescendo, which this piece calls for. By the way, it is not nearly so difficult as it looks!

Exercises are taken from the following pieces:
(1) Andante in D No. IX from "A little Organ Book"
—Charles Wood

(2) No. I from "A little Organ Book"—*Parry*
(3) March—"Crown Imperial"—*Walton*

Note on the history of Organ building.

The history of the building and design of organs is not, strictly speaking, relevant to the scope of this book. If it does interest you to know in more detail how the modern instrument developed, and something of its ancestry, you can easily refer to the books listed in the bibliography. But certain salient facts are important, as they have a direct bearing on your playing and approach to the instrument; and particularly as we have just been discussing the (much abused) Swell box, this is as good a place as any to insert a short historical interlude.

The organ developed much earlier on the Continent of Europe than it did in England. That is why so many stops have German or French names. Indeed the Puritans of the seventeenth century under Cromwell, through their distaste for elaborate music in church, destroyed a large number of organs—or removed them for their own use! But their success in this was not long lasting, since music, particularly organ music, was fully restored along with the monarchy in 1660, and very soon reached new levels of achievement in the work of Purcell.

While this was going on in England, the organ and organ music on the Continent, especially North Germany, was reaching maturity. The instrument of the period is sometimes referred to as the "Classical" or "Baroque" organ, though the two terms are contradictory, and the latter word is perhaps misleading. As it was originally used as a term of derogation to describe the excessively ornamental and sumptuous style in architecture and sculpture of the time, it would be more accurate to refer not to the "Baroque organ", but to the "organ of the Baroque period"—a very different thing. The chief features of it which concern the organist were extreme directness and "bite" in its speech, and very light wind pressure, producing a transparency of tone; all these are the very opposite of the conditions prevailing today. This has a very direct bearing on the way you approach the music of Bach and his predecessors, and the style in which you play it. Clarity of texture between the parts, and rhythmic vitality are felt with much more keenness on such an instrument than on a modern one. And what will your playing amount to without these two ingredients?

As far as organ building is concerned, in Bach's day the

instrument already possessed a complete and independent pedal organ (see Appendix 2); French organs also acquired pedals early; but in England, organs were built without them up till about the end of the eighteenth century, and of course such instruments survived into the nineteenth. But on the other hand the Swell box was an English invention, and was only later incorporated into Continental organs. British builders also led the way, during the nineteenth century, in replacing the old Tracker action, first with the Tubular pneumatic, then later the Electro-pneumatic that we have today.

These points show that when you come to play a piece of organ music written by Bach or one of his contemporaries, apart altogether from the considerations of style which I suggested a moment ago, you would be mistaken to put into it devices of expression such as the Swell box crescendo, which did not exist when he wrote. Moreover, you would expect English organ music written before 1800, to take a round figure, to be for manuals alone. If you come across a piece by a Tudor composer, or Purcell, or Handel (with a few exceptions) or other eighteenth-century composer, with a pedal part, you will know that the music has probably been edited or arranged so as to include it.

CHAPTER VI

SETTING ABOUT PLAYING (1)

*Aims in practice — Essentials of good playing
— Some objectives for practice*

WE have now mentioned all the main parts of the organ—
or should I say those parts that directly concern you, the
player—and discussed some of their chief characteristics.
From the exercises given you will have got the general
"feel" of the instrument, and an idea of some of the difficulties and limitations an organist has to overcome. Before
proceeding further with the business of teaching yourself
how to play, you must decide in your mind exactly what it
is that you are aiming for. I do not propose to give in the
following chapters a fixed and rigid set of rules, by following
which you will emerge at the end, hey presto! as a fully
fledged organist. The important thing at this stage is to
ask the question, "What is the purpose in my practising
the organ? Why need I work at a piece of music in
detail?"

The answer should of course be, "In order to play the
piece well." My purpose in the next pages is to try to discover how that is going to be achieved.

The only thing that will make your practice fruitful, and
will give your work a sense of purpose, is a clear picture in
your mind of what constitutes good organ playing. Such a
picture will give you an ideal to work towards, and every
moment that you spend practising will help in some way to
bring your playing nearer to it. Even the simplest piece
(and what could be simpler than a hymn tune?) can be so
worked at that finally your playing of it comes as near as
you can make it to what it should sound like.

Each time you practise, set yourself an objective, one single point, however apparently limited, and do not be satisfied until you have really got it right. Thus you will always be working consciously towards the goal of good organ playing.

What are the essentials of this? To start with, there must be complete ease and assurance of movement, both of hands and feet. You will never see a good organist worried or bothered by having to manage a complicated box of tricks, or lurching forward awkwardly simply to draw a stop, or losing his poise when he starts playing the pedals. Another fundamental essential is the ability to choose appropriate stops for whatever the piece may be; or to put it more generally, a complete knowledge of the instrument. The only real way to master the organ and to manage its large resources effectively is to understand what it is capable of. In this connection the specifications given in Appendix 2 can be of great help in assessing, for example, what Bach's organ could do. Make a specification of your own organ and study it from all angles. Know its weak points as well as its strong ones.

The third essential in good playing is a sense of style. This covers an enormous range of musical points, and really deserves a book to itself; yet suffice it to say that organ playing which lacks style is terribly tedious. The style of playing appropriate to a Bach Fugue is totally different from that required for a piece by César Franck; the style of a Chorale Prelude is quite different from that of a Fantasia, even by the same composer; again there is all the difference in the world between a Sonata by Bach and one by Mendelssohn. If you play such divergent pieces in the same style, at the same dead level (particularly of registration), your performance will lack an essential ingredient of good playing.

Let me just add what good playing is not. It does not consist of "technique", as some might automatically say if asked to define it. Technique is not something mysteriously

apart from, and separate from, the music, which can somehow be "learnt" independently and then applied to
whatever piece you wish to play. Technique is simply the
way you play; it is inherent in the music itself. So such an
answer is no answer.

People often say—"I heard So-and-so playing the organ,
but I could not say whether it was good or not, as I know
so little about it."

Such an attitude of mind is most commonly found, and it
really covers two extremely important points. The first is
the quality of the music itself. It is true that most people
have no definite idea what constitutes good organ writing.
This is unfortunately proved by the amount of rubbish that
is both printed and played—certainly in this country. But
more of this later when we come to discuss repertoire. The
second point, which vitally concerns us here, is the quality
of the playing. How can you tell what is good playing and
what is not? People somehow expect a different standard
of critical judgment to be required for a performance of
organ music, and assume that the laws and standards which
apply to this instrument are of a different order from those
which apply to the rest of music. Admittedly this may well
be because the ordinary music-lover, having suffered
torments in the local church on Sunday, naturally comes
to expect less of an organist's performance than of any
other performance in a concert hall, and therefore to
gloss over faults which anywhere else he would not
tolerate.

I take it as axiomatic that the organist is in no way exempt
from the standards by which other performers are judged.
Broadly speaking, whether his playing is successful or not
depends on considerations which can be applied with
exactly equal validity to any other musical performance.
He is not the special favourite of St. Cecilia. But naturally
there are certain peculiarities in the instrument which
single it out from other instruments, and which require
special attention. It is these which now concern us.

Let us therefore consider these as some of the objectives which you might set yourself to work for in practice.

(1) Ease of movement at the console, leading directly to complete independence of the various parts of the music.
(2) Clarity of playing—largely as a result of (1).
(3) Fingering and pedalling.
(4) Continuity of performance.
(5) Management of stops, consistent with (4).
(6) Correct volume. For practice pick a quiet registration.

(1) This point may well present the chief difficulty, the more so if you are a comparative stranger to the organ. Practise the parts individually. If you are right-handed then your left hand will need special attention. If you are a newcomer to the instrument, then your pedals will need it too. Therefore the exercises in this chapter are intended to promote independence between the left hand and pedals.

You will probably find that if your left hand moves up (the keyboard, of course) your feet will tend to do the same, and vice-versa. Practise getting used to contrary movement of hands and feet. The way to approach these exercises is to take the left hand part first, working particularly at the fingering and phrasing. Start slowly and gradually get it up to speed. When you have got it as fluent as you can, then try the pedal part by itself in the same way. I have suggested a pedalling to save time. When that is perfectly phrased and in time, then play them together.

(2) Clarity is all-important. Music in which several parts are woven together, in other words, contrapuntal music, is fundamental to the organ; it is no coincidence at all that the Fugue is the most effective organ form. So to play clearly the different parts that go to make up the whole is of the very first importance. It is part of any organist's technical equipment to be able to assess and allow for any reverberation the building may have, so that the parts may

come through clearly. So this is a fundamental consideration for player and listener alike—could you hear what was going on? Was the counterpoint clear, or was the texture thick and stodgy?

(3) Never hesitate to experiment with fingering and pedalling. Take a passage and thoroughly work it out. Then if on playing it through you find it is awkward for any reason, alter it and try again. Do this until you have really become fluent with that one passage, however short it is. You will find that if you set yourself even a limited objective one day, and practise so as to achieve it, doing this will act on your playing as yeast acts on a loaf, and you will find infinitely more interest in the music. Thus if you really solve the problem of fingering (or pedalling) a passage one day—there is no reason why it should take very long—then you can set yourself another objective the next.

(4) This really covers two points, the one growing out of the other. The first is actual continuity of playing (in other words, with no breaks); the second is the continuity of the musical thought behind the playing.

Continuity is the heart and soul of the organ. Any note you press down will sound continuously; therefore an organist must match his playing to that simple fact. You would be instantly aware of it if an organist played something that went in fits and starts, or was in the habit of holding over a note or chord while he carried out a search for the next note to play, or for a stop to pull out! The continuity of musical thought (which both these faults mentioned would violate) applies more the longer the piece, and we shall come to discuss it again under the heading of Registration. But even a short piece, or hymn-tune, must be thought of as a continuous whole from beginning to end. It must therefore be played in one, and the registration and pulse must combine to give the listener the feeling that it is one piece of music.

(5) The management of the stops is a problem peculiar to the organist. The choice of tone-colour is made purely on musical considerations; this therefore is one fundamental way of assessing musically a performance of organ music, and an essential consideration for you, the player— Did the registration sound convincing? Was there sufficient variety? The dictum that "variety is the spice of life" is more valid than ever when it comes to organ playing.

(6) It is the easiest fault to fall into to play too loud. If the stops are there in front of you, the temptation to "let go" is almost irresistible. Yet it must be resisted. Even in the loudest piece always aim to give the listener the impression that the instrument could have given more; never find yourself with every stop drawn and the box open in the middle of a piece! The louder you play the more burden you impose on your own clarity of texture, which as we have just discussed is the first consideration.

Finally, when you practise the organ, particularly if you repeat a passage several times (as you should if you set yourself a worthwhile objective) use a fairly quiet stop for the purpose. You can never tell who may be there listening. If it is a church there may be people in it, or visitors looking round, or cleaners at work, and it can be really irritating to have to listen to someone learning a piece with loud stops perpetually drawn. Of course when you get to the stage of deciding on registration, that is a very different matter; when you are acquainted with a piece then you will be perfectly entitled to launch out and experiment more boldly.

The Exercises are taken from the following pieces:
(1) Fugue in C No. 1 from Eight short preludes and fugues
—*Bach*

(2) No. I from "A little Organ Book"—*Parry*
(3) Psalm Prelude in E flat (Set I, No. 2)—*Herbert Howells*

EXERCISES

Herbert Howells

CHAPTER VII

SETTING ABOUT PLAYING (2)

Fingering — Pedalling —
Balance — Tempo

THE principles on which you approach organ practice are all-important. It is not simply a question of doing certain things, carrying out certain exercises, spending a certain amount of time at the organ. You can easily do all that and more, and still not get any nearer to playing the organ well. The vital element that will make your work interesting and purposeful is the knowledge of the goal towards which it is directed.

In the last chapter I suggested some of the factors that go to make up good playing, and some of the objectives to set yourself when you practise, which will help you towards that goal. One point mentioned was fingering. It is most important that you should not step aside from things which may seem to you unimportant details. Often it is the smallest things which spoil playing. Now we shall discuss others.

The chief objective in the exercises given in the last chapter was independence between left hand and pedals. Quite obviously this is essential; in this chapter the exercises are a continuation of the same principle, applied to right hand and pedals.

Every passage should be fingered (or in the case of the feet, pedalled) as if it were to be played legato. You should vary the speed at which you play the exercises, so that when you play a passage quickly you feel no trace of stiffness or awkwardness. There is no single fingering, or pedalling, that is "right", all the rest being "wrong". The right fingering for you is that one which gives you personally

most comfort when playing. It simply determines the
position of the hand (or foot); if your hand becomes stiff or
contorted when you play a passage, then your fingering
needs altering accordingly. Ease of movement is the chief
factor; everything else is subservient to it. So it is well worth
spending a little time in deciding on that particular fingering,
or pedalling, which is best for you. When practising you
must be sternly self-critical, and not allow any awkwardness to pass you by unchecked.

If a pedal part lies in the upper part of the pedal board
for any length of time, turn your body slightly to the right.
Face the music, quite literally. This will help you to focus
your attention onto it, as it were. If it lies in the lower part,
turn your body slightly to the left. You are thus much more
likely to develop the necessary flexibility of movement than
if you face rigidly to the front.

So if when practising a passage you pick on fingering, or
pedalling, as an objective to work for, you will be doing
more good than is immediately apparent to you. It has far-
reaching consequences. But if neglected, the consequences
will be equally far-reaching—in the opposite direction. Of
course every point you pick is related to every other one,
as they are all ultimately to be brought together in the same
piece of music.

Another objective you can with profit set yourself is the
question of balance. I do not mean your physical balance
on the organ stool, but the musical balance between one
part and another. As we are at this stage considering the
component parts of organ music, and analysing its performance, this is the moment to discuss the need for balance
between the various musical strands.

The aim to keep in mind in this respect should be clear
beyond doubt. If the three fundamental parts (Right hand,
Left hand, Pedals) that go to make up the music are of
equal importance, then none of them should be too quiet or
too loud, relative to the others. If one is too quiet it will
not be heard in equal degree; if it is too loud it will obscure

the other two. Moreover, if one of the parts starts by itself, it should not be played with such penetrating stops (even though by itself it is just tolerable) that when the other parts are added the result is deafening.

But if one part is a solo part, then it must be heard distinctly above, and apart from, its accompaniment. The accompaniment must not be so loud that it steals the show.

Very often the pedals need very careful attention from the point of view of balance. The bass part needs to be firm and satisfying. As already discussed, the pedals if coupled to a manual will operate any stops drawn on that manual, together with its own. Care is needed to ensure that an overloaded pedal part does not spoil the musical effect of the whole.

To play with the correct balance between the various parts is of such importance that it is difficult to overstress it. The larger the organ, the greater the choice and variety of stops, the closer the attention you must pay to it. It is not simply a matter of the quantity of sound, in other words the volume, of the different stops, as of their different tone quality. You should aim at the earliest possible moment to get to know thoroughly the tone quality of all the stops that are available on your instrument.

Such questions as the following need to be both asked and answered. If I change from Great 3 to Swell 3 is there a violent change in volume? What difference does it make if I have the Swell box open or closed for this transition? If I wish to use a Stopped Diapason (8′) on the Great as a solo stop, what stop(s) do I need on the Swell to provide a suitable accompaniment? Have I any stops on the Great or Choir which would provide accompaniment for a Swell reed, (a) with the box open, (b) with the box shut? Assuming that my only pedal coupler in use is Swell to Pedal, what Pedal stops are needed with Swell 3 to provide a satisfactory, and not too loud, bass line? And so on; in other words you must fully know your organ.

So much for balance. There is another fundamental

question that requires a decision on the part of an organist before he begins to play even the simplest and shortest piece; in fact before he plays one bar; a question all solo performers have to answer; namely tempo—the speed at which you are going to play a piece. By varying the speed of the exercises, you should have begun to develop a flexibility in your approach to this vital matter. This is another objective for you to set yourself in practice—really establishing and maintaining the tempo which you consider to be the best from all points of view. It is certainly one of the first criteria of a solo performance.

The organist has more considerations than other solo performers to bear in mind when deciding on speed. Of course one of the best ways of finding the right one is to experiment, and find it by trial and error. What is the right one? That tempo which gives you comfort, allows the music to be clear and the organ time to speak, is not so slow that it stands still in its tracks, nor so fast that it becomes a scramble, and which produces the required effect in the particular building in which you are playing. The best tempo for a small organ in a small building may not necessarily be right for a larger organ in a larger building. A small scale performance with relatively few stops, all sounding directly with negligible time lag, in a building with little or no reverberation can well afford to be taken at a faster tempo than a performance of exactly the same piece of music on a larger organ with greater resources, probably greater delay (between the time the note is played and the time the sound reaches the listener) and in a building of greater size and resonance. One of the essential qualifications of a good organist is that he should be able to adapt his playing in this way, and to play a different organ in a building of different character at a moment's notice. Do not therefore allow yourself to become too tied to one particular instrument; see whether it is possible for you to move about and play other organs.

Stops have different speaking speeds; that is to say some

take longer than others for their sound to be effectively produced. A sharp-tongued reed will have a quicker speech than a dull-edged flute; a low 16' pedal note will take longer to speak than a note of higher pitch; a pipe far away from the console will take longer than one close to it. These points are of particular importance when it comes to playing staccato Pedal notes. Do not play them so short that the notes, especially quiet low ones, have not time to speak, nor so long that they cease to be staccato. You might with great advantage make this your single objective for one practice: take whatever piece you happen to be working on, and decide on the tempo purely from the point of view of allowing the quieter notes time to speak effectively, with whatever stops you have decided to use. Compare the first exercise at the end of Chapter VI, with that at the end of Chapter X.

Your own comfort of playing is not a subject which can be taught here; you yourself are the best judge of the ease with which you play something, and you can best decide if the tempo you have chosen is quicker than you can manage.

Again, the tempo you choose for a piece must allow for clarity. In the last chapter we discussed continuity, variety, clarity; I have little doubt that the greatest of these is clarity. It can suffer terribly if the tempo is too fast. If you are in fact teaching yourself, your musical instinct and ear will be your only guide in this matter—unless you have heard a good performance of the piece you are playing, and even that may not necessarily be a sure guide; it may have been given under totally different conditions from those prevailing when you play. So that throws you back simply onto your musical instinct. For the exercises I have put in a metronome mark to help you. If you look at the pieces from which the exercises are taken, decide whether my suggested tempi are satisfactory. In some copies you will find speeds marked; take them as a rough, general guide (for an average organ in a building of average size) rather than a final rule.

C

There is however one most useful "rule" which will help you in deciding tempo; that is to fix your attention on the notes of smallest value. They will probably be semiquavers, but they may be demi-semiquavers. Never play a piece so fast that these notes are lost, even though they are only the small change of musical currency. They should be as distinct as you can reasonably get them. A good example of this is the opening of Mozart's Fantasia in F minor, where the small notes must be distinct and definite.

It will be evident from this that if you decide to play a passage of semiquavers with a stop of dull, slow-speaking quality, the tempo you choose must be correspondingly slower; otherwise the definition will be lost. The semiquavers for example in a Bach piece must be always perfectly distinct. The size and resonance of the building in which you play will be a most decisive factor in deciding tempo. In a fairly small church the time taken for you to press the key and the sound to reach the listener is almost negligible. In a larger building it may be as much as a second, and of course the sound will linger after you raise your finger from the key; so more time will be needed for the whole process, and the tempo at which you play will be adjusted accordingly.

So we have established some more standards by which to judge good organ playing, and I hope suggested some more objectives for you to set yourself when practising, all of them contributing to the ultimate goal. Practising really requires a stern discipline. As we have discovered you must first set yourself a target to work for; then keep your attention focused on that, not allowing it to be distracted by the innumerable things about the organ which may do just that; finally you must be exceptionally self-critical, and not imagine that you have achieved what you set out to achieve after the first five minutes!

The following exercises are now intended to develop independence between the right hand and feet—the first most fundamental need. The basic aims we have been discussing in this chapter—fingering and pedalling, balance, tempo—will of course apply at all times.

The Exercises are taken from the following pieces:
(1) Andante from Sonata no. 3 in A major—*Mendelssohn*
(2) Fugue in E minor No. 3 from Eight short preludes and fugues—*Bach*

EXERCISES

CHAPTER VIII

SETTING ABOUT PLAYING (3)

*The need for anticipation — Memory — Preparing pedal entries
— Melodies played with the pedals — Double pedalling*

You must appreciate that every reader, every player, will
have a different problem, and that therefore all these
chapters can hope to do is to suggest general principles.
Individual problems can only be solved individually—in
fact having got so far in the process of self-instruction you
will be very well advised to continue your studies under a
good teacher—but the general principles of variety, clarity,
continuity, independence of parts, balance of parts, tempo,
are fundamental to all organ music, in fact to all music, and
are therefore of prime importance to understand.

I have suggested exercises first to develop independence
between left hand and pedals, then between right hand and
pedals. Of course these short extracts are only models of
what you should do with any and every piece you choose to
play; the more you practise, the more fluent you should
aim to become; but do not think that as soon as you have
sorted out these short examples you are then ready to tackle
anything. All they can do is to start you working towards
the right goal. It would be most advisable for you to take
the pieces from which they are extracted and go on from
there, applying the same principles to the whole.

If you are to play a piece successfully, and manage your
instrument well (which is a *sine qua non*), apart altogether
from simply playing the notes, your mind must continually
be on the alert, and particularly you should be able to
anticipate different points before reaching them, and thus
to give yourself time to prepare. If you know that there is an

awkward change of manual at a certain point, or that the
Swell box needs to be opened in order to effect a smooth
change-over, or that a certain stop change is particularly
difficult, or that the fingering of a certain passage is difficult
—in such cases you are able to prepare for and meet the
difficulty only if you know what is coming beforehand.
When you reach the later stages of learning a piece, you
can with great profit set yourself that objective. Select the
first and most obvious problem of organ management that
the piece presents, and quite deliberately see whether by
working it out beforehand, and by anticipating the difficulty
while playing, you can negotiate it with ease.

In many ways this is similar to driving a car, when it is
of great importance to anticipate what is coming. If you
know a particular stretch of road you will naturally drive with
much more confidence; you will know that a certain part is
not nearly so dangerous as it appears, and you will therefore
not put on the brake, as someone might who did not know
the road. Again you will know that further on there is a
sudden steep hill, or some other trap for the unwary, and
will drive accordingly. It is entirely a question of knowing
what is coming and dealing with it in advance.

And just the same with organ playing. When driving you
should never become so preoccupied with the dashboard or
the gears that you fail to see an approaching danger; when
playing you should never become so engrossed in the copy
that you do not see what is coming round the next turn.
While practising you should continually feed your memory,
and make it your aim that after a certain while you are able
to play a piece, or even just part of a piece, without the
copy. This involves not only playing the notes but also
managing the instrument from memory.

I do not know at all how the human memory works, nor
how your sub-conscious mind acts on your conscious mind,
but I do know that it is not nearly so difficult as you might
think to memorise short stretches of music. If you practise
a section thoroughly one day with particular reference to

certain points which seem to you difficult, you can return the next day—or even the next week—and find that your mind has somehow assimilated those points. The art of memorising is to memorise the way a passage goes, and the way you play it, not to memorise the notes parrot-wise. Of course your ability to memorise what you play largely depends on how many other distractions you have, and how long you are able to spend at the organ. But if you set yourself the task of developing the ability to play from memory, you will agreeably surprise yourself; it seems far more difficult and frightening than it really is.

We have thus established another criterion of good organ playing—memory, and particularly the art of anticipation. When listening to an organist's performance, you may not have been able to see whether he used a copy or not. The best performances are from memory entirely, not because it is "showing off" (more often than not the organist is invisible) but because it means that the player has studied, learnt, assimilated the music, and that his mind and imagination are so developed that he is able to reproduce it himself. To put it another way, he is able to play subjectively from his feeling and understanding of the music, rather than objectively, from simply watching the printed page.

But as even the finest player cannot memorise more than a certain amount, it is unreasonable to expect this always. Even when using a copy a good organist will not be "glued" to it; he will simply use it to help his memory as and when needed—though, of course, he will already have anticipated all the various points of difficulty, and decided how to deal with them. The greater the musician, the more he memorises.

Perhaps the most usual case when the need for anticipation is greatest is in the matter of pedal entries. Have you ever allowed an entry of the pedals to come upon you unawares, so that you have had to scramble and dig and hope for the best? Or have you ever been playing, intent on the manuals and the copy, and then realised that the pedals were supposed to have come in several bars previously?

The pedals need preparation, so that the movement of the music is not held up when they are added. When you play on the manuals alone you may quite easily have to use the Swell box, and your right foot will in that case be on the Swell pedal. This you must on no account think of as being a permanent fixture; when the pedals come in, the feet—both feet—should be there ready to play. If it is necessary to turn the body to right or left—in other words if the pedal part lies particularly high or particularly low—you should anticipate this movement in plenty of time, so that when the moment comes your feet are absolutely poised and ready to play.

While on the subject of the pedals, there is one vitally important point to discuss. The pedals need not necessarily have the bass part. In England we have been brought up to think of organs as massive instruments producing immense gushes of sound; it is surely clear that in such circumstances the more volume your instrument produces the firmer must be your bass line to support it. It is because of this that we have come to think of the pedals as primarily 16' stops, which either provide the bass line or remain silent for an occasional respite, and which are almost inevitably coupled to whatever manual is in use.

I do not mean to suggest for a moment that the pedals are not really supposed to provide the bass part. Of course they are, and in nine cases out of ten they do. But what about the tenth case?

Imagine that you are writing a piece of organ music (and what better way is there of teaching yourself the organ?) which is going to be based on a hymn-tune. This tune consists of fairly even notes of long duration, largely minims. Round it, on top of it and underneath it, you are going to work the other parts, which are going to be given quicker-moving, florid passages of quavers. By doing this, the bass part (by which I mean the lowest part) is going to consist of quavers. How are you going to lay that out for the organ?

The pedals are notoriously unsuited by their very nature for quick passages, unless it is a solo in bravura style, particularly if any scales are involved. All they can do with any comfort is the sort of passage found in Ex. 4, page 44. Surely it would be much more suitable to give the main tune, with its longer notes, to the pedals, give the lowest part to the left hand, the other to the right hand? If you do that, remember two things; the pedals should be left uncoupled, otherwise they will interfere with the other parts, particularly on a Tracker action instrument, where the manual key is actually played when coupled to the pedals; also, as they are uncoupled, they must have a sufficiently carrying 8' tone; no 16' of course, otherwise the bass part in the left hand will be clouded. See whether you can discover a Chorale Prelude of Bach built on this pattern, with the pedals (uncoupled) playing the main tune in the tenor part.

The pedal organ of a good instrument should have a wide selection of interesting stops, which would make such a piece as the one just described a practical proposition. If your instrument just has the usual 16' Bourdon of course you should not attempt it. But an interesting pedal organ should also have 8', 4', even 2' stops; possibly also mutations and mixtures. It should have fairly quiet yet colourful reeds, and not merely be content with the usual deafening and unwieldy Ophicleide, with its excessive wind pressure more than the rest of the instrument. Bach's organ at Leipzig had only one flue stop on the pedal organ, the rest being reeds. (See Appendix 2.) Buxtehude's organ at Lubeck had a most comprehensive Flue chorus (32', 16', 8', 4', 2'), and an almost equally comprehensive Reed chorus (32', 16', 8', 2'), and a mixture as well, on the Pedal organ.

You may also have found certain pieces in which the pedals have two notes to play at a time. Octaves in the pedals are of course, quite easily negotiated (practise playing a scale in octaves with the feet); but if the pedal part is divided into two, each foot going its own separate way, you would be well advised not to attempt it, at least for the present.

So now on to the next stage of exercises, which aim primarily at independence between the three different parts. Play them, as before, singly first of all, then two parts together, then all three. And do not forget to vary the tempo.

EXERCISES

The Exercises are taken from the following pieces:

(1) Fugue in G major No. 5 from Eight short preludes and fugues—*Bach*

(2) Fantasia in F minor and major—*Mozart*

(3) Chorale Prelude on "O Lamm Gottes Unschuldig" from the "Orgelbuchlein"—*Bach*

EXERCISES

C*

CHAPTER IX

REGISTRATION

General points — Limitation of dynamic marks — Violent changes to be avoided — Reeds and their use — Registration to coincide with phrasing — Stops decided by the character of the piece — Two specimens

REGISTRATION, or the art of choosing what stops to use, is peculiar to the organist, and a matter of the greatest importance. No other player has such a wealth and variety of tone-colour at his disposal. The simplest piece can be made a work of art the moment you use an imaginative registration; in the same way, a fine piece can be ruined by dull registration.

Some general points first of all. It is true that "anything can be mixed with anything", and constant experiment with different combinations of stops is essential. But in the first stages, clearly differentiate between the different "families" of stops. Refer again to Chapter II. Suppose you have a quiet, smooth-flowing passage, for which you consider Swell flutes would be effective. Eight-foot tone by itself always sounds rather monotonous after a while, so you look for a 4' to go with it. Imagine that your organ has not a 4' Swell flute (which is more than likely). Try the Swell Octave. If you have not that either, you may find a 16' stopped Diapason; that would be perfectly good, and you would then play the passage an octave higher. Failing that you could use the Principal 4', or Fifteenth 2' with quite good effect. 8' and 2' tone together (without the intermediate 4') are often very colourful and effective.

Never rely on the combinations that the pistons give you. They can always be altered, and they are certainly not a sufficient substitute for thinking out your own registration, and adding or taking away stops by hand.

One of your greatest difficulties is the interpretation of the various dynamic markings. When all is said, there are only six markings, possibly eight, for the entire span of volumes, from the lowest to the highest, irrespective of the character of the music.

$$(ppp), pp, p, mp, mf, f, ff, (fff)$$

The following gradation marks are also used:

> Louder: Crescendo, più f
> Quieter: Diminuendo, meno f·

So a passage marked *f* in one context may well be utterly different in both volume and tone colour from one marked *f* in another. A flexible approach to this matter is essential, as well as individual imagination.

To take just one illustration, if you see a passage marked "Swell, *p*", any of the following would be reasonable, depending on the circumstances:

(a) Celeste 8′ by itself—if the passage comes at the close of a quiet piece, and represents a falling off in volume.

(b) Flutes 8′ and 4′, if it is a lyrical passage of some length.

(c) Full flues, if the passage comes as a contrast to a louder passage (on the Great) just before it, and you therefore require something fairly firm, though quieter by comparison.

(d) Full Swell with the box shut, if the piece is of a brilliant nature, and the quietness is of only temporary importance, soon to give way to something of a different character; or if the piece is so short that to take off reeds (assuming that they are already on) would cause too much disturbance.

Generally speaking, if you need to change from Great *f* to Swell *p*, you should not have such quiet stops on the

Swell that the music disappears from view completely, and the listener has to grope about for the sound. Never make too violent changes either way. It should be clear that it is of little use a composer laying down specific stops to be used, as every organ and every building is different. César Franck marks his scores as much as anyone, though he leaves a tremendous amount of discretion to the player, who must in his turn aim to reproduce the general effect as closely as he can on his particular instrument.

A special word of caution is needed about reeds. The larger and more resonant a building, and the greater the space surrounding the organ, the more the tone of the reeds is mellowed and rounded off. But in an acoustically dead building, reeds sound more "edgy" and direct, largely because a higher wind-pressure is needed to counteract the deadness. So reeds should be used sparingly. The more sparingly you use them, the greater effect they will have when you do. Sometimes when playing fairly full, with the Swell box shut, you can add the Swell reeds and hardly notice them; then gradually open the box, and you have a really vigorous and effective crescendo. But never add them suddenly, with a sudden harsh impact.

Any quiet reed, even a chorus one, makes an effective solo stop. Do not rely on the few obvious solo reeds that are usually available on the Choir organ. When deciding on accompaniment for a solo stop, it is not necessary to confine yourself to 8′ tone by itself. What makes a solo predominate is not only its greater volume but also its more individual tone colour. It is not advisable to try to make a solo from a stop of the same family as the accompaniment, as it will not be distinguishable from it. For example, if you play a solo with the Tuba stop, the accompaniment needs to be firm enough to match it. But it would be inadvisable to choose the Full Swell, as the Tuba is itself a reed; much better take a Flue combination, if possible on the Great (assuming the Tuba is on the Choir), as this will be the most satisfactory. If on the other hand you wish to use the Swell Open

Diapason as a solo stop, the obvious accompaniment would be Choir (or Great) flutes. You could in that case use the Swell box to adjust the balance as need be.

Constant fussing when you are actually playing is inadvisable, as it tends to break up the natural flow of the music. You have to strike a balance between altering something every other bar, and altering nothing at all throughout a piece. It is a fairly safe general rule that you should never push in or pull out a stop if by so doing you cause an interruption in the music. The movement of the music is the first consideration.

Arising out of that, any alteration you make must coincide with the music's movement; you should aim to make your alteration of stops either at the beginning or at the end of a musical phrase, never in the middle. You can imagine the equivalent in speech, if you were to break into a shout for the last two syllables of:

God save our gracious queen.

It would come over to the listener as:

God save our graCIOUS QUEEN,

and would naturally sound comical. It would also sound just as comical if you were to drop your voice suddenly:

GOD SAVE OUR GRAcious queen.

Whatever tone-volume you start with needs to be maintained through to the end of the line; of course this does not rule out the gradual crescendo or diminuendo.

If you are going to build up the volume, start the increased tone-volume at the beginning of a musical phrase, where a break would not sound unnatural. Examples of adding stops and taking them off will be found in the two examples given at the end of this chapter. Notice where the changes occur, particularly with reference to the phrasing.

The choice of stops should coincide with the nature and

character of the piece played. It is impossible to give any hard and fast rule, and every piece has several possible ways of registration. But always aim to understand the character of the music. The heaviness of stops you choose is also related to the tempo at which you play the piece. The heavier and thicker the tone, the more time it will need to be effectively heard.

When you have become acquainted with the particular organ you play, you will get to know the positions of the various stops; then if you want to add a stop at any particular moment you can fix your eye on it in advance, so that you avoid any feeling of being rushed or bothered when the time comes.

The principle on which to approach the problem of registration is perhaps best illustrated by the formula "variety with continuity". Nothing is more deadening to organ music than a monotonous registration; yet you must not be so fussy that you break up and destroy the music's continuity of movement. Moreover, the degree of any build-up you make must be decided with an eye on the dimensions of the piece; if it is out of proportion, one way or the other, that will also help to destroy the music's continuity.

I shall now give a registration for two simple pieces which you might easily take as a starting point. They are the first piece, by Parry, from "A little Organ book"; and No. 4 of Eight short preludes and fugues, by Bach. (For publishers see Chapter XI.)

(1) *The first piece from "A Little Organ Book"—Parry*

This is marked "tranquilly", straight away giving a valuable clue to its character. It is quite short, only 32 bars, so that there is not room for any violent build-up. The only suggestion of f is qualified by "poco" (bar 26)—in other words not too much. Two manuals, Swell and Great, will be enough. Obviously you will start on the Swell.

Notice that bars 9–16 are a note-for-note repetition of

bars 1–8 as far as the hands are concerned, the addition of
the pedals being the only difference. So at bar 9 you would
add something to the Swell; 4′ probably—anything so long
as it is not too violent a change. Reeds, need I say, are out
of the question in a "tranquil" piece.

For the middle portion of the piece, starting at bar 17
(the half-way mark), you would play on the Great, in order
to give a feeling of something fresh—but coupled to the
Swell, otherwise you will not be able to work a Swell box
crescendo. The middle section represents a sort of minature
"development section", based on existing material. You
will not need the Great to Pedal, as when the pedals come
in again (bar 23) you will be back on the Swell.

So at the beginning prepare Swell to Pedal, Swell to
Great; Pedal—soft 16′; Great—Stopped Diapason, or
Dulciana 8′; Swell—8′ Flute, or Diapason.

Bars 1–4. Start with the box shut, and work a small crescendo in bar 3. The "dim" can be lengthened to coincide
with the end of the phrase in bar 4.

Bars 5–8. The main difference here is more crescendo
effect with the Swell box. It will probably be about half
opened in bar 5, fully opened in bar 6. Again the drop
back can be lengthened, though remember that your
right foot is needed for the pedal entry in bar 9; do not
get so carried away that you leave it too late!

How are you going to add any stops in bar 9? Both hands
are fully occupied, and we will rule out foot-pistons, as
your organ may not be blessed with them. But notice that
the lowest note in the left hand (E♭) coincides for one and
a half beats with the pedals, which are coupled to the Swell
in any case. Why duplicate unnecessarily? Your right hand
therefore, takes the upper left hand notes as well as its own
(which is perfectly possible, and quite easy), your pedals
take care of the E♭, and your left hand is thus left free to
draw the necessary Swell stop, which in most cases will be

situated on the left-hand side of the Console. Having drawn the stop, it can then resume its normal place of duty. You should make a break between bars 8 and 9 in order to clarify the phrasing.

What stops you add depends entirely on the organ; but the important thing is to feel the need to add something. You may have a piston giving you Diapason and Principal, which would be perfectly good and provide an effective contrast to the Flute tone you have just had. You may even have a quietish 2-rank mixture, which would not be impossible, though you would need care. A 4′ Flute, or Octave, are the obvious choice.

Again it would be possible to go onto the Great straight away at bar 9, first preparing Great to Pedal if you are going to do this. That would mean keeping nothing but 8′ tone up till bar 16—slightly questionable in a piece of only 32 bars, but just possible. You might find a change of manual easier to negotiate than a change of stops, and, as we have found, ease of movement is essential. But you would need to add something in bar 16 (last beat, where the left hand has a crotchet rest) and also take off Great to Pedal in time for bar 23. On the whole I am in favour of staying on the Swell until bar 16; but I mention the alternative to show that it is impossible to lay down one single registration. Supposing that your organ has only one manual, you would then have to decide in which bar it is more important to add something, bar 9 or bar 16!

Bar 17. Great without pedals. The first Swell box crescendo must be very gradual, as you now have 4′ tone on the Swell; aim for a broad, spacious crescendo to match the phrase in bar 19, followed by a gradual dim.

Bar 21. The next crescendo is obviously less. On the last beat of bar 22 there is a sequence starting on C♭, marked p. There is no better way of underlining this than by changing to the Swell. In the next bar the same phrase is repeated with different harmonisation. So take off the 4' on the last beat of bar 23, lifting your hands to underline the phrasing.

Bar 24. Return to the Great at the "a tempo". You need to be there for the passage marked "poco *f*", and the last beat of bar 24 is the point where this long phrase starts. You should not suddenly add volume half-way through a phrase. The Swell should be gradually opened as indicated.

Bars 27–end. By bar 29 you need to be back on the Swell, as that is where the 4-bar Coda starts, based on the opening 4 bars. Where is this change of manual going to come? Bar 28 will also have to be Swell, as the two bars (28 and 29) are tied together. That brings us to bar 27. It all fits perfectly if you change to the Swell in accordance with Parry's phrasing, in other words on the second beat of bar 27. There is another reason why this is the best place. To repeat E♭–C of the previous phrase in exactly the same way would almost amount to tautology; the moment you put the second occurrence of these notes onto a different manual it makes the passage much more interesting.

The final four bars are a good example of a gradual reduction to pp. Do not reduce to the realms of the inaudible too soon.

(2) *Prelude and Fugue in F—Bach*
    (No. 4 from "8 Short Preludes and Fugues")

Again we will assume that yours is a two-manual organ, and confine ourselves to Swell and Great.

Remember that for Bach the Swell box is an anachronism, and there are only the choice of stops and manuals to make the music live.

Prelude

The piece falls into three sections:

Bars 1–14. These consist of a fanfare-like opening of 4 bars, followed by ten bars, in which Bach introduces the main material of the piece.

Bars 15–44. Three episodes make up this section, with cadences in D minor, C major, A minor respectively; they are built from the material of the opening.

Bars 45–end. These consist of a restatement of the opening.

This short analysis should show you that the last 14 bars are going to have the same registration as the opening 14 bars; any variation is going to come in the middle section.

What is the character of this piece? Think of it as Allegro moderato—fairly bright, at a moderate speed, the parts perfectly clear, as otherwise the effect of the counterpoint will be lost. It consists largely of the interchanging of right and left hands; therefore have your two manuals uncoupled, with stops of roughly equal volume but of contrasting tone quality. For example:

> Great: Flutes, 8′ and 4′
> Swell: Diapason, Oboe, Principal 4′ or Fifteenth.

You will need to experiment with the Swell box to find out where to set it in order to hear both parts equally. The Fifteenth (2′) will perhaps be better than the Principal (4′), as both the Oboe and the Diapason are on the solid side. Only use the Oboe if your organ has a fairly smooth one. If it is of the raucous variety, leave it alone and use something else.

If your pedal organ has 8′ and 16′ of sufficient tone to sustain the other two parts, then you can leave the pedals uncoupled. Otherwise draw a soft 16′ and couple Great to Pedal.

Bars 1–4. Both hands Swell. The quiet reed is just what is needed to catch the listener's attention to these introductory bars.

Bars 5–11. Left hand Swell, right hand Great.

Bars 12–14. Great both hands, to round off the opening section.

Bars 15–22. Left hand Swell, right hand Great. Notice that the figuration of the notes is changed round from what it was in Bar 5; this time the right hand has the quavers, the left hand the semiquavers.

Bars 23–28. Both hands Swell, because both hands have the same figuration, and the music is more homogeneous.

Bars 29–34. Both hands Great.

Bars 35–40. Right hand Swell, left hand Great—in contrast to bar 15.

Bars 41–44. Both hands Great, to round off the middle section.

Bars 45–end. An exact repetition of Bars 1–14.

By means of the interchange of two manuals and a handful of stops, we have managed to extract both interest and variety from Bach's score. Stop changes are thus superfluous.

Fugue

This can be taken on one manual, the Great. It is too short to consider introducing "Episodes" on the Swell. Couple Swell to Great and take off the Swell reed that you used for the Prelude. On the Great substitute an Open Diapason for the Flutes. More pedal stops will be needed to match this; be sure to draw Great to Pedal. The time taken for these adjustments should be as little as possible! No change in registration will be called for in this fugue, at least until bar 23, as the variety and interest lie primarily in the parts themselves. In bar 23 there is a rest after the first beat, just before the pedals have the main subject again, with the left hand in thirds. You would be perfectly justified in adding something here—Swell reed and Mixture perhaps, or Great Principal and Fifteenth. Always bear in mind the degree of volume you wish for your final chord. The piece should come to a firm ending, with reference to what has gone before. Do not be one of those who aim to pull out everything in sight just for the last chord! Even in a much longer piece, such an attitude is questionable.

CHAPTER X

RHYTHM. AND PHRASING

Rhythm foreign to the organ — The meaning of rhythm — What makes playing rhythmical —. Use of the Metronome — Causes of unrhythmical playing — Making notes belong together — Different ways of phrasing — Pedals to be phrased as well as the manuals

(A) Rhythm

THE organ is the most unrhythmical instrument there is—with the possible exception of the bagpipe. That is to say, rhythm does not come naturally to it, and unless the player is alert it will not oblige.

There are several factors contributing to this. The steady flow of air made possible by the "reservoir"—a feature shared by organs and bagpipes!—produces an even, steady flow of tone, with the result that the organ naturally prefers a sustained sound to one that is broken up. Then again, the tone is ready-made; the organist does not have to create his tone quality as a violinist or a pianist does—it is all done for him; and although this does not automatically make the instrument unrhythmical, it does tend to make the player lazy. After all, he can control a vast range of different tone-colours simply at the press of a button. So be on your guard against laziness. But a feature which most decidedly does make the organ a problem rhythmically is the cumbersome, mechanical nature of the instrument, which even the most efficient electric action cannot entirely outweigh. In many cases the player is working by remote control, with or without a sound-lag, and it all contributes to make vital, rhythmical playing difficult to attain.

Rhythm has to be imposed on the organ externally, as it were, to a far greater extent than in the case of other instruments. But imposed it must be. Therefore, because un-rhythmical playing is the most common of faults, let us first define rhythm, and thus get a clear picture of how it affects organ playing.

Rhythm primarily means patterns or formations of notes, each note being separate and distinct, but together adding up to something of musical meaning. Two notes are the minimum required for a rhythmic pattern; of course those two notes could be the same note (i.e. in pitch) repeated. See Ex. 1 at the end of this chapter.

But the word also has a deeper meaning, one which is of the closest concern to you as a player. If you define Tempo as simply the speed at which you play something (which is what it is), then rhythm is humanised, or vitalised Tempo. It is what makes a musical phrase continuous and logical; it makes one phrase balance (or rhyme) another; it makes the listener want to hear more, by leading him forward through the music which moves logically with correctly placed accents. These are sometimes called "agogic" accents—very aptly, since they represent points of arrival in one phrase, points of departure in the next, and drive the music inexorably forwards. But such accents are quite foreign to the organ, and have to be deliberately imposed by the organist. A good example of this is to imagine a row of six quavers in front of you. Play them

(a) as if the piece were in 6/8 time.

(b) as if the piece were in 3/4 time.

You will notice that the only method of establishing either rhythm on the organ is to introduce a slight sense of "loitering" on the strong beat. In other words, you make this longer (therefore stronger) beat into an accent, a point of departure for that bar.

The best way to establish the rhythm in your mind is to hum the phrase through to yourself. With that picture in your mind, you can use it to assert your musical will, not of course over the music itself (your job is to recreate the composer's intentions, not to rehash them), but over this particular blank spot of the organ. Provided that you have a clear, vivid picture in your mind of the way a musical phrase should go, from its beginning to its end, it will be hard for you to play it unrhythmically.

Single notes have no meaning; but in association with others they make sense. Rhythm is that element which decides how you shall progress from one note to the next; it is the vitalising element which binds them together and makes them coherent. The closest parallel is an ordinary sentence, in which the single words mean nothing if they are not spoken in association with each other. When that sentence is spoken rhythmically, in other words with the right degree of movement and "agogic" accent, and without any arbitrary lumps or bumps, the meaning of the words will emerge.

The organ will try to tempt you into believing that single notes have a meaning by themselves; you will then, by listening to individual notes, lose sight of where the phrase is going to which they belong. The only possible remedy for this is to imagine the whole phrase as a rhythmic unity before starting to play; and do not allow yourself to be led astray by the sweet sounds coming from your instrument.

So Tempo by itself is not everything; but it is certainly something, and something closely related to rhythm. You must pick a speed that gives time for the clear articulation of any rhythmic patterns there may be. So often organists play in such a way that notes become merged into each other and lose their identity. You must take into account that notes of low pitch are more difficult to "manage" rhythmically than higher notes. Try a rhythmical pattern with the pedals, and see what care you need to get the notes articulate. It is not simply a question of varying the Tempo; by doing that it is possible to alter the whole character of a piece.

First decide on Tempo. That will then be your norm, which must be firmly established before any "rall." or "accel." will have any validity. If the music changes speed at any point you must decide in advance, before you start playing, the speeds of the various sections. Do not whatever happens leave it to the whim of the moment. Most editions have metronome marks suggested at the beginning; these are only a rough guide, and do not excuse you from making your own decision.

Having decided the Tempo you then have to decide the "layout" of the various phrases that go to make up the sections. To take as an example the Parry piece that we were discussing in the last chapter, the first four bars make up one phrase, answered by the next four bars. Now if the second phrase is taken slower or faster than the first, or the balance is in any other way disturbed, the result will be unrhythmical. Rhythm consists partly in rhyming one group of notes with another; any superfluous slowing down —which the organ would be only too delighted to do given half a chance—will upset that rhyming, and produce unrhythmical playing. In a fugue, therefore, you must clearly establish the tempo which best suits the fugue subject, and then maintain it. Naturally every entry of that subject must be at that tempo (including the pedal one), unless there is a very good reason to the contrary. As an example of this sort of exception, Schumann marks some of his fugues "poco a poco accel."; or rather "nach und nach Schneller"

That brings me to consider your most present help in times of trouble, the Metronome. Use it, but let it be your servant, not your master. If it is wrong that a fugue (for example) should be taken at an absolutely strict and unwavering tempo, at least it is a fault on the good side. Far better that than play it in such a way that your tempo is not really established even when you get to the end. The Metronome can give you an unwavering beat which is of the greatest help, particularly when you are in the fairly early stages of learning a piece.

There are also other vital ways in which it can help your

musicianship. If a piece is in 4/4 time, and you come to some bars consisting largely of crotchets or minims, in other words your fingers are not having a lot to do, the most natural tendency is to speed up. Conversely, if the music then breaks into quavers or semiquavers, you may feel a strong temptation to slow down and allow the fingers more time to manage the greater number of notes. Or perhaps you may be one of those whose alarm and despondency at the sight of a "black" passage, when you have just come through a "white" one, transmits itself to your fingers, and causes them to play quicker and more nervously. In all these cases the metronome will enable you to keep the pulse regular.

But never lose sight of where the music is going. To sum up, the basic cause of unrhythmical playing is twofold:

(1) Inability to memorise, or visualise, a complete musical phrase.

(2) Inability to manage the instrument in some purely technical way.

(B) Phrasing

Rhythm and phrasing are inseparable. As we said, notes only have a meaning when played in association with each other; it is phrasing which determines which notes are associated together, and how. If you refer again to the Parry piece that we discussed in the previous chapter, you will see that Parry has given exact instructions how the various notes are related to each other.

If you hum the opening four bars (as you should before playing them), it is impossible that you should think of the notes apart from their correct phrasing. The organ, as already mentioned, has very few devices of "expression"; the Swell box is the most obvious one that springs to mind. But the only "device" as far as manual technique is concerned, apart from changing from one manual to another, is to lift the hands at whatever points are necessary to show the phrasing and the shape of the music generally. Lightness or heaviness of touch itself, as we found, are immaterial.

Take just one bar to illustrate this point, the first bar. The first two notes in the right hand belong together; they will therefore be played legato, as the slur indicates. But the second note will be shorter than the first; and the third note is separate. Therefore between the second and third notes the right hand is raised from the key as much as is needed to produce the required effect.

Notes 4, 5 and 6 also belong together. Naturally a slur placed over a group of notes means that they are to be played legato, without raising the hand at all between them. But here Parry wants the 5th and 6th notes to be short, so he has to counteract the legato implied by the slur by simply putting staccato marks over the notes. This

rhythmic pattern: is quite fundamental,

and occurs throughout the piece. If you have a clear mental picture of it, you should then play rhythmically. But it is quite impossible to have a clear image of this pattern if you think of it merely as notes divorced from their phrasing.

Moreover, this characteristic rhythmic pattern occurs so often in the course of the piece that if you play it with the correct phrasing you should feel a tremendous sense of variety, even of accent, the moment the phrasing includes four quavers spread over two beats (bar 19); or four notes spread over three beats (bars 26/27).

When you come to play Bach, you find that the decision about phrasing rests largely with you, as he left no indication in the score. There are countless different ways of phrasing the same passage—"different combinations of dots and dashes". The important thing to realise is that some decision is necessary. No one today can tell you whether you are "right" or "wrong", only what they think. If your pronunciation of a musical sentence is based on thoughtful musical judgment, you are just as likely to be right as the next man! (See Exercise II.)

Phrasing and registration are most closely allied. When altering the registration, do so at the beginning of a phrase. This is a most useful way of underlining the shape of a passage. The simplest example is a hymn, in which the addition of stops can bring out and accentuate the meaning of the words.

Finally one very important point. The pedals must be phrased as well as the manuals. You can even afford to exaggerate the phrasing with your feet by lifting them earlier, and leaving the natural resonance of low notes to carry the tone on. In a fugue, the subject must have the same phrasing when it is given out by the pedals as it had when given out originally.

EXERCISES

The Exercises are taken from the following pieces:

(1) Concerto No. 2 in B flat—*Handel*

(2) Fugue in D minor No. 2 from Eight short preludes and fugues—*Bach*

EXERCISES

1 RHYTHM

CHAPTER XI

ORGAN MUSIC

The isolation of the organ — Reasons for this — Three consider-ations in assessing organ music — Disregard of the organ by greatest composers — Characteristic organ music — What should organ music do? — Lack of living tradition — Suggested repertoire

WE have discussed the various parts of the instrument, as far as is needed for practical purposes; we have mentioned some of the chief points to bear in mind when practising and playing; now we must consider what music there is for the organist to play.

The principle which I followed in Chapter VI I shall again follow here; in other words I do not propose simply to give a list of pieces which I personally think are "good", and leave it at that. Instead I think it will be of much more interest to try to suggest some standards by which organ music as such (irrespective of its performance) can be judged. You cannot be held responsible for the music there is to be had; but you most certainly can be held responsible for what you choose to play. How do you choose what to play? This question is not nearly so easy as it appears.

First it is necessary to bring organ music into some sort of perspective. Although the history of the organ goes back an extremely long way, the course of music written for it runs rather separate from that of the rest of music. The connec-tion between the organ and the church is inevitable, and something of the same secluded separateness surrounds organ music. It accounts for the deep-rooted, traditional conservatism which naturally tends to separate organists from other musicians, and makes them focus their attention backwards onto what is old and "safe" when the prevalent attitude among their colleagues in other branches of music is forwards onto what is new and ambitious.

But now the church no longer represents the centre of gravity of our music; that has been transferred to the concert-hall. Moreover, it certainly is not the case that everything old is automatically "good" and interesting, everything new is automatically suspicious if not bad, any more than vice versa. The question is not nearly so simple as that.

The comparative isolation of the organ is made more marked by the fact that its full tone, made up of an immensely wide harmonic range, does not reproduce well either on gramophone records or on the radio. Its harmonics do not like being topped and tailed for purposes of transmission, and the ordinary loud-speaker or gramophone cannot reproduce more than a suggestion of the original. The full effect of an organ can only be heard in the building itself where it is played. Without doubt this has adversely affected the popularity of organ music.

All this is of extreme importance when you come to decide what is good and effective organ music. All of us subconsciously (if not consciously!) tend to like what we know and are used to, and thus to imagine that we know what we like! So do not immediately assume you know what is good organ music because you have heard a few recitals and like some of the pieces that were played.

There are three fundamental questions to be answered before deciding whether a piece is worth your attention. Was it written by a front-ranking composer? Is it suited to the organ? Does it achieve what (presumably) it set out to achieve?

It should be clear beyond question that if a piece of music is written by a composer of the front rank (even in an off-moment) it is far more likely to be worth your attention, and to repay your study, than a piece by a composer of less standing. This rather obvious statement is of basic importance when considering organ music, since it is an unfortunate fact that composers of the front rank since Bach, with certain exceptions whom I shall list in a moment, have ignored the organ almost to a man. This neglect naturally created a vacuum in the organ repertoire, which composers of less worth have been only too ready to try to fill.

The cause of this neglect of the organ lay, I believe, in the fundamental aims of the greatest nineteenth-century composers, which were broadly speaking the development of· tonality and key-relations, and the development and expansion of the symphony and symphonic form. But whatever one may pick out as being the chief characteristic of great nineteenth-century music (if indeed it is possible so to generalise) it was without doubt a period of expansion in every way. Unfortunately for the organ, its limitations are soon felt; its characteristic music is contrapuntal (that is to say written in different parts), and it is not really a coincidence that its most effective and greatest music (some think its last great music) should have been written in an earlier age when counterpoint, rather than harmony, was the order of the day, and by a man who was himself an organist and contrapuntalist par excellence.

As I say, the result of the post-Bach neglect of the organ has been a flood of poor quality organ music. The great composers failed to provide works, so organists had to provide them themselves. Music lovers today to whom the term "organ music"—as represented by recitalists—means such names as Rheinberger and Boëllmann may therefore be excused if they are disposed to wonder whether the organ has its own peculiar scale of musical values, applying only to itself. Can poor music become less poor if it is played on the organ? Of course not; music is either good or not, for whatever instrument it is written. But the modern organ is unique in that it can produce a full, luscious tone, and continue to produce it in such a way that the listener has his senses drugged as it were. The sheer sound can be overwhelming. Nevertheless, the music must be judged as music; and there has been proportionately more rubbish written for the organ, and printed, and played, than for any other instrument. So you must be wary, and not accept the first thing you come across.

What front-ranking composers wrote organ works after Bach? Mozart out of all his vast output wrote two (and some works for a small instrument), which are played with embarrassing frequency by organists. Mendelssohn wrote some fine sonatas, as well as some preludes and fugues. Schumann wrote some extremely beautiful and intimate fugues on B.A.C.H. (in German B is B♭, A is A, C is C, H is B♮) as well as other pieces for pedal piano. He was no organist, and his pieces therefore need rather careful handling. Brahms wrote some rather dull fugues, but also some of the finest Chorale Preludes to be found. Bruckner, though an excellent organist, wrote as far as I am aware only two short pieces. But for the high water mark of the nineteenth century we must go to France, where César Franck produced and played most individual and effective organ music, without having recourse to the vulgarity of his contemporaries; unfortunately the genius of this most individual French master was not passed on to his successors Widor and Vierne. Perhaps his individuality was too pronounced.

Nevertheless the French school continued, and continues, unbroken, and represents today a unique phenomenon of musical activity. No other country can boast a greater interest in, and concern for, the organ and its music. Messiaen particularly has written most vivid and colourful music, certainly the most personal since Franck. Alain also has left some most moving and effective pieces. There is no doubt that this last composer's untimely death in 1940, at the early age of 29, cut short a most strikingly original and deep-thinking musical mind, and is a serious loss to organ music.

In England Parry fought nobly, if self-consciously, for the revival of English music, against impossible odds from across the Channel. English music had lain dormant for more than a century, and he had little to fall back on apart

D

from the Wesleys, or Sterndale Bennett and one or two
others, so who can blame him if his works have the familiar
flavour of Brahms about them? Even so, some of his organ
works are well worth study. Elgar wrote, among other pieces,
two organ sonatas, the second of which is infinitely better
than the first, although actually it is an arrangement of the
"Severn" Suite, which was composed as a test piece for
the 1932 Brass Band Festival at the Crystal Palace! More
recently, Vaughan Williams has written a handful of short
pieces, Rubbra only one.

From elsewhere the story is the same. Sibelius has written
two organ pieces out of his whole output; Hindemith three
Sonatas. But there is an interesting, even exciting exception
to the general rule to be found in the work of the Danish
composer Carl Nielsen. He wrote 29 preludes for Organ,
and one full-scale concert piece called "Commotio". His
music has tremendous originality, and is exceptionally
well written for the organ. It is not surprising that we find
him declaring that he ignored the intervening years and
modelled his writing on Bach. (What the intervening years
did for the organ we shall discuss soon.) As we say about
Mozart, if only. . . .

What about pre-Bach composers? First and foremost of
course, Buxtehude, whom Bach once walked 200 miles in
order to hear. His music is extremely effective, some of it
fairly simple. The Dutchman Sweelinck was a master who
exercised considerable influence; so in a lesser degree did
the German Pachelbel a century later. In England Purcell
wrote some fine pieces, and the keyboard works of earlier
Tudor composers can in some cases be played on the organ.
In the eighteenth century, Handel was an organist of
tremendous repute, as well as a composer of eminence, so
that his music can usually withstand the customary arrangement. Indeed his Concertos sound almost as effective when
played simply as a solo as they do with String Orchestra.
Generally speaking eighteenth-century English composers
(e.g. Stanley and Boyce) have a freshness about them

which is admirably suited to the organ. Yet nowhere is the poverty of the organ repertoire more clearly shown than in the field of the Concerto; until quite recent times, the organ concerto stopped with Handel.

How is one to decide whether a piece is suited to the organ? This question really means deciding what is characteristic organ music; what is the essential quality of good organ writing.

Music for the organ consists essentially of a melody, an accompaniment and a bass; three parts; three equal, independent, interwoven parts. I do not mean of course, that the word "melody" should be taken in the popular sense, but simply in the sense of a melodic line of notes— as for example a Fugue subject. Obvious examples of characteristic 3-part writing are the Organ Sonatas (or Trio Sonatas) and Chorale Preludes of Bach, and most of the organ works of César Franck. (For example Prelude, Fugue and Variation; Pastorale.)

Most Fugues are in 4 parts, but there are some fine examples of writing in more than that number. The part played by the left hand when it is in the nature of an accompaniment (in the stricter sense of the word) will probably have more than one single line of notes; other notes will be needed to fill out and complete the harmony.

But always beware of thick chords. The reason for this can easily be demonstrated. Take a chord of three notes and draw stops of 8', 4' and 2'. What is the actual sound that chord will give when you play it? The 4' stop will give you one octave higher, the 2' stop two octaves higher from what you play. So what sounds will be this:

Nine notes for the price of three! Obviously if you add to that another similar chord in the left hand, and something or other in the pedals underneath it all (16′ remember), you are going to get a thick, muddy texture, which if prolonged will be intolerable to a sensitive ear. Not to use 4′ and 2′ stops, to say nothing of mutations and mixtures, is no solution to the problem. If you do that you simply deprive the organ of its chief source of character and colour, and take away its depth of tone. Try playing something with only 8′ stops in use. For a time, particularly in a quiet passage, it is uncommonly effective—especially if it is used in contrast to what comes before or after; but very soon the need for variety is felt.

The extension of harmonic experiments in the romantic period of the nineteenth century culminated with the lush chromaticism of Wagner; the expansion of the orchestra itself can easily be seen by comparing the size and the instruments required at the beginning of the century with the enormously increased numbers and more developed instruments in use at the end. Organ builders followed suit, and their products became larger and noisier than ever, intended to produce an "orchestral" sound. The organ in the Royal Albert Hall, London, originally built in 1872, is I suppose as good an example as any of this sort of development.

But the organ is not, and never will be, an "orchestral" instrument, still less a "romantic" one. The fundamental difference lies in the fact that an orchestra achieves its build-up by combining different sections—strings, wood-wind, brass, percussion—each section contributing its characteristic tone. For instance, the tone-quality of the Brass section is characterised chiefly by Horns, Trumpets, Trombones, Tubas; that of the Woodwind section by Flutes, Oboes, Clarinets, Bassoons; together all the sections combine in a Tutti which is a bringing together of these diverse elements and tone-colours. The organ achieves its build-up by combining the different parts (i.e. Soprano, Alto, Tenor, Bass), each of which has the same tone-colour. It is contrapuntal not harmonic. So organ music that is written on an "orchestral" or "harmonic" basis, probably with thick, full chords, can hardly fail to sound stodgy and terribly monotonous.

Thick chords, marked f or ff, with or without "wrong" notes for the sake of modernity, are only tolerable for a very short time. A chord by its nature tends to stand still; organ music is essentially contrapuntal, in origin choral, and its interweaving parts keep the music moving.

The strong romantic predilection for sheer weight of sound, as exemplified in the works of Berlioz or Strauss, may or may not have produced orchestral works of brilliance; opinions vary—in any case such a point is beyond the scope of this book; but it is invariably fatal in organ music. Nevertheless not very long ago organists used to include in their recitals unwieldy transcriptions of orchestral works. Even now some new organ works are headed "original", as though that is the last thing you would expect in such a composition!

So much for your decision about the extent to which a piece is well written for the organ. You must next decide whether it achieves what it set out to achieve. In this matter it is perhaps difficult to free yourself from prejudiced (I mean pre-judged) ideas about what organ music should do, what it should be.

If a piece of music sets out to entertain you and it does so, then it is successful; if it sets out to instruct you and it does so, then it is successful; if it sets out to fill you with a sense of joy, or beauty, or misery, or reflection, or any other emotion, and it does so, then it is successful. When deciding about a piece of music it is necessary to decide what were the composer's basic motives and intentions in writing it in the first place. In a large number of cases it seems that pieces written for the organ have been intended either to be "easy", or to produce an atmosphere of artificial piety, quite removed and apart from the outer world—just as organ music as a whole has been becalmed in a backwater, away from the mainstream of the rest of music.

To composers of such insulated music, religion has become mere religiosity, legitimate sentiment has degenerated into sentimentality. The result is a serious disservice to the organ, as it lowers its stature as a musical instrument—one capable of effective musical speech—and to the organist, as it gives him no credit whatever for artistic judgment. Such pieces are usually given tempting descriptions—"short", "easy", "simple", "quiet". But any piece that is worth your time to play requires the exercise of your musical thought and study and imagination. If you wish for fairly short and simple pieces, there are enough by front-ranking composers to keep you busy!

So the principles on which you decide what pieces to play are not so straightforward as they might have appeared at first sight. Nor—which makes it more difficult for you, I am afraid—will you get much help from other people's opinions. Go first of all for the composer himself. Is his music original or secondhand? Is it vital? Is it intrinsically suited to the organ? What was his purpose in writing? Did he succeed? It is clear that you will not base your decision primarily on whether the music is old or new, though this consideration may help you to decide whether an idea is original.

As an instance of this, take the Chorale Prelude. Bach did not invent this particular form, though he did carry it on to a higher pitch than any of his predecessors. By what means did he achieve this? First he knew and loved the hymn-tunes on which they were based; he also saw the deepest significance in the words that went with them; thus they acted in him as the spark which ignited his musical imagination; he then brought to bear on them the full weight of his musical armoury—which is saying something. Parry did much the same thing on a smaller scale with the well-known hymns of the Anglican Church. So did Charles Wood with tunes from the English and Scottish Psalter. But today how can the Chorale Prelude be anything but a nostalgic copy of the original? The very name is a relic!

For sheer musical value, your time is best spent with the original.

Which is a most disappointing state of affairs. It means that there is today no living tradition in organ music, and that the prevalent trend is traditional—not by any means the same thing. The active imagination of the greatest creative musicians has been directed elsewhere, and the organist has had to pick up what few crumbs he can from the rich man's table, or else go below stairs where there is a great deal to be had for the asking! It was natural that, being denied works by front-ranking composers, organists should take the next best thing, and inflate its value. But this does no service to the organ.

The need for every student and lover of the organ to exercise musical discretion and taste is both urgent and paramount. He should honestly assess everything he hears and plays; and by refusing to be content with the third-rate he will contribute in the greatest possible way to the creation of a genuine living tradition of organ music.

LIST OF WORKS SUGGESTED AS A BASIS FOR REPERTOIRE

(Those marked * are fairly easy)

	Publisher or agent
16th and 17th Centuries	
Buxtehude. Complete works*	12
English Organ Music. "Tallis to Wesley" series .	12
Pachelbel. Organ works	5
Purcell. Organ works	5
Sweelinck. Echo Fantasia (2 staves) . .	12
Variations "Mein junges Leben hat ein End"	11
Tallis. Funeral music*	6
Various composers. Italian organ music* .	12

18th Century

English Organ Music. "Tallis to Wesley" series .	12
Handel. Organ Concertos (Ed. Marcel Dupre)* .	11
Mozart. Three works for the organ . . .	5
Various composers. 80 Chorale Preludes of the 17th and 18th Centuries*	12

Of Bach's works, a number are of an easier standard than the rest. It is impossible to be rigid, but
the following are suggested as suitable for those
of limited technique:

> 8 Short Preludes and Fugues
> Certain Chorale Preludes (Orgelbuchlein)
> Little E minor Prelude and Fugue
> Fugue in D minor—the Giant
> Fantasia in 5 parts

Certain other Preludes and Fugues are fairly simple.

19th Century

Brahms. Organ works*	4
Bruckner. Two pieces for organ	12
Franck. Organ works	11

Easier than the rest are Cantabile, Pastorale,
Prelude, fugue and variation.

Mendelssohn.—Organ works	11

Certain movements of the Sonatas are simple.

Schumann.	6 Studies for Pedal Piano, Op. 56 .	2
	4 Sketches for Pedal Piano, Op. 58 .	2
	Fugues on B.A.C.H., Op 60 . .	12

20th Century

Alain.	Trois pieces pour grand orgue . . .	11
Elgar.	Sonata No. 1, Op. 28	4
	Sonata No. 2 (ed. Atkins) Op. 87A . .	13
	Suite for organ (ed. Mansfield), Op. 14* .	1

Hindemith. 3 Sonatas	8
Howells. Psalm preludes (2 sets) . . .	5
Messiaen. Organ works	11
Nielsen. 29 Preludes*	7
Commotio	12
Parry. 7 Chorale Preludes (1st set) . . .	5
7 Chorale Preludes (2nd set) . . .	5
Reger. Organ works.	12
Rubbra. Meditation.	10
Sibelius. Intrada	7
Tippett. Prelude (to the Vespers of Monteverdi) .	8
Various composers. A little organ book* . .	1
Walton. March—Crown Imperial* . . .	14
Vaughan Williams. Three Preludes* . . .	9
Wood. 16 Preludes (2 vols. of 8) . . .	9

(Certain ones are quite simple).

Excellent for the beginner is

The progressive organist (ed. C. H. Trevor), in 3 vols.   3

Numbers refer to the following publishers or agents:

1. Ascherberg, Hopwood & Crew
2. Augener
3. Eekin.
4. British & Continental Music Agency
5. Novello
6. Curwen
7. Chester
8. Schott
9. Stainer & Bell
10. Lengnick
11. United Music Publishers
12. Hinrichsen
13. Keith Prowse
14. Oxford University Press

CHAPTER XII

VARIOUS ORGANS

*The cinema organ — Its chief characteristics — Its purpose —
Cinema organist's technique — Reed organs — Their limitations
— The electronic organ — Its theory and practice — future
development*

1. The Cinema Organ

WE have so far discussed "the organ" under that one
general heading; but the genus has several species. The pipe
organ, as found in churches and cathedrals up and down
the land, is the original, the oldest. From that stem, several
varieties of instrument have sprung. The most popular is
the cinema organ. In what way does this type of organ
differ from the other? What peculiarities has it for the
aspiring player?

In Appendix 2, I have included the specification of the
organ in the Odeon Cinema, Marble Arch, London. This
will give you at a glance an idea of what you would be
confronted with at a large console. There are several
fundamental differences between such an organ and a
conventional church organ which are of close concern to
the player. First, the cinema organ is built on the "unit"
principle; this is of importance to understand, as the tone
produced is of an individual nature.

Take one family of stops on an ordinary instrument; for
example the Flute. As we have found, in order to build up
a chorus, you would use stops of different pitch, but of the
same family; perhaps 16′, 8′, 4′; each stop would have its
own rank of pipes, and each pipe would be so voiced by the
builders as to produce a blend of tone with the rest. The
"unit" principle simply gives each sort of stop one rank,

but extended downwards and upwards to cover the 16' and 4', and any others. In this way one rank of pipes may have several stop-keys on the console. Because the rank is thus extended the word "extension" is sometimes used instead of "unit".

The reason for this system is largely economical; in its sparing use of pipes it saves both money and space. But it is clear that what is gained in this way is lost in depth and dignity of tone. Not in volume—that is a very different thing; but in the tonal build-up that is the chief characteristic of the church organ. But of course it is necessary to remember that the two have a very different job to do.

The console of a cinema organ is invariably detached, usually movable. There is never any time-lag in the action, which is electro-magnet operated and therefore instantaneous. The acoustics of the cinema are exceptionally dry, and quite free from any resonance—an important consideration for the player.

The basic stop, which in an ordinary organ is the Diapason, in the cinema organ is the Tibia. The manuals are not, as we have hitherto found, the Choir, the Great, the Swell, but (from the lowest upwards) the Accompaniment, the Great, the Orchestral, the Solo. To those who feel that one Tremulant is an excess (page 20), it may come as a shock to see that the particular example I have specified has no less than ten. It is perhaps the most characteristic feature of the instrument that every section has its own Tremulant. There is also to be found an astonishing variety of Percussion stops, ranging from tonal ones (in other words with notes of varying pitch), to non-tonal ones (sounding only at one pitch). Examples of the first are Xylophone and Glockenspiel; examples of the second are such effects as drum-rolls, cymbal-clashes, castanets, sleigh bells, bird whistles, and many others. These latter are called "traps".

Perhaps the most important distinguishing feature of the cinema organ is the principle of "second touch". By this means, certain stops only sound when the key is pressed fully down; thus it is possible to play both a melody and its accompaniment on the same manual, even with one hand. The stops giving the accompaniment sound on the first, the lightest, touch; the solo stop sounds on the second touch. This principle is also found on the pedals, thus enabling the player to accent certain pedal notes.

The pistons are exactly similar to those found on a church organ, each manual being provided with its own set. These can be pre-arranged to give whatever stop-combinations the organist requires. There are two balanced Swell pedals, which operate just as we have already discussed to give a crescendo. Nor is there anything unusual about the couplers, which join together the various manuals and pedals.

So much for the instrument. What approach should the player adopt who wishes to study its performance? The various principles suggested so far in this book, also apply, generally speaking, to the cinema organist. But from the very nature of the instrument, and the reason for its existence there are some considerations that are only applicable in the theatre. Let us first discuss these, then try to discover any peculiarities of technique the cinema organist needs to acquire in order to meet them.

The purpose of the cinema organ is to entertain the public. This eliminates, with one fell stroke, at least one very real difficulty which confronts his church colleague—namely the choice of music. The cinema organist has one fixed and immovable criterion by which to judge the merit of music before playing it—is it popular? He is not primarily concerned with music of any particular sort or school, but only with music that has an immediate popular appeal. His staple fare is light music, both vocal and instrumental. As he is so much in the public eye, he must be up-to-the-minute with the latest tunes. One moment he may be asked to lead community singing; then again tunes from films, particularly if they happen to be in Cinemascope and Technicolor, have a way of "catching on", and he will have to be able to fill that need. But he must on no account think of the tunes he plays as a joy for ever; popular taste is notoriously variable, and what is "in" one week may well have been superseded the next.

In what way does this affect the organist's technique? One important facility he must develop is the ability to play from memory and by ear. This can be self-taught to a very large extent. Take any tune that comes to your mind, and hum through it mentally. Next do this again, but this time while you are humming, see whether you can understand and follow the fundamental harmony that goes with it. The next step is to go to the piano and see whether you can reproduce the tune with its attendant harmony. You will find that most popular pieces and tunes have a quite simple harmonic basis.

Moreover the ability to improvise is of importance. If you have perfect pitch—in other words if you can identify any note you hear played or sung—then so much the better. In any case, practise playing "ex tempore", confining yourself to short periods at first, since an organist is often required to do that. He is also called on to transpose—to play a song or piece in a different key from that in which it was written. This means that you need to understand the harmonic basis of the piece, and apply it to whatever the key in which you are going to play. (See Chapter XIV.)

In the case of an orchestral work, the cinema organist plays from the "Piano-Conductor" score. His aim is not to reproduce note for note what is written, but the general effect in terms of the organ. Crisp, staccato pedal playing, and tunes well brought out are what the cinema-going public expect.

Perhaps the best summary of what is needed in a cinema organist is that his playing must represent, to the management of the theatre who employ him, a business proposition; he must provide what the majority know best, and therefore like, and thus "hold" his public. And let no one underestimate the hypnotic if sentimental effect of a "mighty Wurlitzer"; or Compton or Moller for that matter. There is one very obvious reason why this particular instrument is suitable for "request items"; it is a one-man band if ever there was one, and therefore involves much less trouble and expense than hiring an orchestra to play. Gramophone records are not quite the same thing, particularly for short extracts. But apart from its expediency, the Cinema organ has a strong popular appeal, and is therefore used; nevertheless fewer cinema managers are now giving employment to organists, and very few new instruments are being made.

2. *The reed organ*

The enormous advances made recently in all branches of scientific technique have naturally been reflected in organ building. It is a truism that the discovery of a new technique does not necessarily go hand in hand with the ability and knowledge how to use it; but there must be experiments, and so far as the organ is concerned there have been some remarkable ones.

Apart from the pipe organ there are two main species of organ in use today—the reed organ, and the electronic organ. Before jumping to any conclusions about these two distinct and separate off-shoots of the organ family, it is necessary to have a clear picture of their lineage. Because they are both given the honourable name of "organ", one may reasonably expect the sort of tone associated with the organ; when that is not forthcoming, one's immediate reaction is unfavourable—"It does not sound like an organ to me." To judge the instruments now to be discussed perfectly impartially, try to forget temporarily the sound made by a conventional instrument, and (if it helps) call the new ones by another name—any other name except "organ". It is difficult to see what other name you can find, particularly as these instruments have a perfectly ordinary console, and are played like any other organ. But various makers evidently felt the need, and produced some colourful names. The important point is that you should assess the result entirely on its merit.

The reed organ derives from the nineteenth-century harmonium. The principle is the same as that used in the mouth organ, or "harmonica", and the accordion. The reed is free—that is to say it vibrates freely in its aperture, thus distinguishing it from a reed stop on a pipe organ, in which the reed vibrates against one edge of its aperture. Air can be either blown, as in the case of the harmonium, or sucked, as in the American organ. You may well have come across the Mustel organ, or the Estey organ; there are several other types.

Their limitations are numerous. A monotonous, slightly anaemic quality of tone, a lack of range, and (particularly in the case of the harmonium) slowness of speech all contribute to make the performance of any rapid or extended passage out of the question. Only the simplest pieces can be attempted. On the other hand, for reasons of economics and space (if the building is small) such instruments have a good deal to be said in their favour. You may know of small remote churches where it has been found that a harmonium provides just the accompaniment needed for simple hymns and other singing. Generally speaking, the best results are obtained in the quieter dynamic range; the player would be well advised to cut his musical coat accordingly, and not attempt to imitate a larger instrument.

3. *The electronic organ*

With the electronic organ we enter an entirely new field. As it is a fact (known to the Greek, Pythagoras) that sounds and numbers are related—as you can see by the alteration of pitch caused by altering the length of a pipe or string—and that a sound can be measured in terms of vibrations, or frequencies, it was perhaps inevitable that sooner or later an instrument would be produced that would do away with pipes as the means of tone-production, while at the same time possess a range of sound comparable to that produced by a pipe organ.

The console of an electronic organ is exactly similar to

that of any other organ, with stop-keys (not draw-stops), pistons, pedal board, Swell pedal and so on. Originally the means of tone generation consisted of oscillating valves, but as it was found that these were unreliable, requiring a great deal of attention, particularly with the tuning, they gave way to an electro-mechanical system. A disc is rotated close to a stationary plate, and by this means an electric wave is produced, made to correspond to the tone-colour required by means of grooves of different shapes incised around the disc. There are twelve such discs, one for each note of the scale, which rotate together, at whatever speed is needed to produce a particular frequency vibration. The range of frequencies required is roughly from 32 cycles per second for low notes, to 10,000 for high notes. The tone generator unit can be placed in any convenient place in the building where it is out of the way; the only other apparatus is the sound producer unit (loudspeakers). So once more, in a building of limited space, this instrument has an advantage.

I have described briefly the means of tone production since its instantaneous, mechanical action has a direct bearing on the player's approach. Apart from the tone, the chief characteristic is extreme sensitivity of touch, and particularly of the Swell pedal—far more than is generally found with pipe organs. The slightest touch can be detected, and the crescendo continues until the pedal is fully pressed down. The variety of dynamic range thus available is very considerable, but it needs most careful use to avoid awkward lurches in the music.

As before, the most satisfying results are in the quieter registers. "Full organ" effects with reproduced tone are bound to be limited, not in volume but in roundness and completeness. A loudspeaker cannot give the characteristic "build-up" of a pipe organ.

When you consider the long history of the organ, the electronic is a comparative newcomer. In spite of its acknowledged shortcomings, it is often used as a matter of convenience; for ordinary purposes of accompaniment of singing it will usually pass muster. But clearly there will continue to be developments in this technique of tone production, as there have been in the last thirty years. The organist of the future will then be invited to pass judgment on instruments of a new kind. Let him do so purely on results—whether the tone is sufficient for the job in hand, both in quantity and quality; whether the instrument can be used not only for accompaniment but for solo work; whether it can be used not only for a small selection of works, but for organ music of all periods, old as well as new. For in the last resort it is not so much the look of an instrument that matters, or the mechanics of its working, but the effectiveness and the beauty of the sound it produces.

CHAPTER XIII

ORGAN ACCOMPANIMENT

*Two types of accompaniment — Firm lead necessary for unco-
ordinated singers — Choir needs support — How to accompany a
choir — Special care needed for psalms — Playing under a
conductor — Co-operation*

ASSUMING that you have worked through the various stages
along the way, and (if you were a beginner) have achieved
the ability to play simple tunes and pieces continuously and
in time (very important, that last point), you may quite
easily find yourself asked to accompany singing of one sort
or another, in church or elsewhere. All the principles suggested so far apply to organ accompaniment.

There are two distinct varieties of organ accompaniment,
and it is most essential that you should decide as soon as
you can into which category you are being asked on any
occasion to fit. The first sort is that accompaniment which
is needed for a group of singers, however large or small in
number, who have not trained and rehearsed together,
whose volume may be immense or negligible, but whose
invariable characteristics are raggedness and lack of
coherence. In such a case the only unifying element is the
organ, and it is therefore the first duty of the organist to
give a firm lead which all present can both understand and
follow. Into this first category I place community singing,
hymn singing, any singing by an audience or congregation,
large or small, who are not led by an effective choir.

By "giving a firm lead" I mean two things; first that the
organist must choose stops of sufficient weight to carry and
be heard by all present. That probably will involve an
Open Diapason, with some 4′ stops to give additional tone.

It is no use whatever being timid and faint-hearted, particularly at the opening. Also the organist must play rhythmically. In the case of a hymn, it is most important to play over the tune, completely or in part, exactly at the speed at which it is going to be sung. Once having started the verse, after allowing a moment for the singers to pick up the very first note, that speed should be maintained. You may well imagine that by maintaining a strict tempo you will leave everyone straggling behind you in wondrous disarray; if you listen to them for the first few lines, that is indeed what it may sound like; but you should not worry. A good, steady pulse is infectious, and if you maintain it, you will gradually lead your congregation or audience into it. In fact, if you once begin adapting your tempo to suit what you think is theirs (although it is most unlikely that they will have one), you will find a similar adjustment will be needed almost immediately; and so the downward process will continue.

Unless you provide the necessary lead, the effect will be lifeless. Once the rhythm is established, the organist can afford to vary or reduce the registration, but not before! In the case of a hymn, it will probably take at least two verses for the singers to feel and establish the regularity of the beat.

The second category of accompaniment is that in which there is a choir, trained and rehearsed together, who are in the habit of singing rhythmically and decisively, and thus giving the lead that is necessary. In such a case your accompaniment will be of a different order. Your aim must be to support the choir, not push it; still less drown it. There has grown up what almost amounts to a tradition that the accompaniment of any choral work, whatever is supplying it, should drown the singers. You can hear it in countless performances by choirs and choral societies, who struggle against unequal odds. Of course, the singers must not be swamped by their accompaniment—the very word "accompaniment" proves that.

Your registration should be both colourful and imaginative. So you would not maintain a ceaseless 16' pedal, such as might well be needed for the first category of accompaniment. Never play so loud that you cannot hear the choir; the choir should never have to "force" their tone in order to be heard. If your organ has a Choir manual, this is exactly the purpose for which it was intended.

Generally speaking, reeds and mixtures should be used sparingly. In the first category of accompaniment they can sometimes be added with great effect to make an impressive climax; in the second category it is well to remember that a reed, with its comparatively harsh, incisive tone, makes a poor support for a voice—particularly a boy's voice. In fact the voice has to compete against it. Flue stops are much kinder to a choir. But occasionally the Full Swell, with the box shut, gives a most effective variety. The art of accompanying a choir is a matter of exercising musical judgment in matters of tempo, rhythm, variety, registration, phrasing, balance. Always experiment intelligently; always listen.

If you are accompanying a choir, you are providing the background against which they sing. The organ must on no account be allowed to pull them back; your registration should be guided by the words being sung as well as by the size and quality of the choir, and the nature of the building. In this way you can as it were dot the i's and cross the t's of their singing, and help to make it infinitely more effective.

To put it another way, you must by your playing invite the choir to give their very best. It is not simply a matter of avoiding playing too loud or too soft; that is a purely negative approach. A full-blooded tone, if played in its correct context, musically led up to, and properly phrased and managed, need not necessarily sound too loud. In the same way, the quietest stop you can imagine, if played unrhythmically and without reference to what the choir are singing would not be too quiet; in fact it would not be quiet enough! Nothing is more unmusical than a vague background noise—which probably, if analysed, turns out to be our old friend the Voix Celeste or Vox Humana.

Such playing is of no use to any choir, who need a definite if imaginative accompaniment.

The first category of accompaniment is really the more difficult, as you are asking the organ to do what it so dislikes doing—to play rhythmically. But in the case of a hymn, if you think of at least the first line as a rhythmic unity (see Chapter X), you will probably play it as such. You will certainly avoid the more glaring faults that unthinking players fall into; for example, starting the tune with one note before the rest; or leaving a foot firmly embedded on one pedal note and forgetting about it! Whatever tempo you choose for a hymn, your decision will be made partly in consideration of the number of people there (a larger number will necessitate a slower speed and a fuller tone), partly according to the nature of the hymn itself, and the mood of the words.

Let us consider one of many possible ways of accompanying a hymn—for example, "The head that once was crowned with thorns", to Jeremiah Clark's fine tune "St. Magnus". We will assume there is a choir of moderate ability, a congregation of moderate size. The mood of the words is obviously one of rejoicing; let your registration be correspondingly bright. Verse 1, Great to Principal, coupled to Swell to Fifteenth. For the next verse the words "The highest place" suggest something more—therefore add mixture or reeds on the Swell, making sure that the box is shut to start with.

By this time the rhythmic movement of the hymn is either established or not. Let us hope it is! So for verse 3 reduce; simply Great 8' (mf), without the Swell coupled, would be effective. Verse 4 hands alone on the Swell, with Open Diapason and Reed 8' for a contrast. This can be maintained throughout the verse, since four lines is not too long. For verse 5 a solo (Great), either in the Tenor or the Treble part. If you introduce a solo in the Tenor range, it is important to have 4', even 2' tone, as well as 8'; the latter by itself, unless it is a really powerful Tuba—suitable only for very large occasions—would not come through as effectively.

The last verse would probably be Great to Principal (or Fifteenth), with the Swell coupled; a fairly substantial volume to balance the opening, and finish in a confident mood, as the words do.

The tempo you choose should be cheerful but not trivial. The tune has a real feeling of dignity if the tempo is not too fast. "Moderato" would be the best marking ($\quarternote = 72$). There is no need for any breaks; note values should be observed absolutely, particularly between the second and third lines. This will give the music an impressive, dignified movement. Think of lines 1 and 2 as really one line, and on no account should there be any pause between them.

The accompaniment of psalms needs a special mention. The need to play the chant through in time is surely self-evident; yet it is astonishing how many organists fail to do this. If you do not set your choir an example of time-keeping, how can you expect them to sing rhythmically? Yet the vital point to remember is that the chant is not a strait-jacket in which the words of the psalm are to be imprisoned. It is the chant which, throughout the psalm, must be moulded to fit and suit the words, and not vice versa. All the various psalters aim in their different ways at realising the rhythmic flow of the words—some with greater success than others. But the salient point to realise is that every verse of every psalm has its own special rhythmic movement (see Chapter X). Therefore the bar-lines in the Anglican chant must not be adhered to when singing the psalms; two strict beats in a bar are quite alien to the relative freedom of psalm rhythm, or speech rhythm. If you assert the bar-lines you upset radically the natural word movement. And this is particularly important to remember when accompanying; the organ must fit the rhythmic movement that the choir should set up in their singing. If it acts as a dead weight, dragging the words back as it were, it can effectively kill the singing of psalms.

Generally speaking, a light accompaniment is advisable, with sparing use of the pedals. Psalms (and canticles) are without doubt the severest test of an organist's ability to accompany singing.

PLAYING UNDER A CONDUCTOR

What has been said above about organ accompaniment applies equally well to playing under a conductor. You may be providing the only accompaniment, or you may be playing in association with an orchestra. In either case certain special considerations need to be borne in mind. Your playing must always be with the beat. That means noticing the sort of beat the conductor gives, and any peculiarities or mannerisms he may have. Notice the speed of reaction to his beat on the part of those he is conducting. Do they react at once, or does it require several attempts, with or without explanations, before his intentions are conveyed? Can you see the baton comfortably from where you sit? There should be a mirror conveniently placed so that you do not have to swivel round awkwardly every time you want to see the beat. That simply means you will never look!

Notice particularly the preparatory beats; by that I mean the preliminary movement that a conductor carries out before he gives the executive beat, or the word "go". From this preparatory beat it should be possible for you to feel and judge the tempo he has chosen. The need for anticipation is never more essential than in such a case.

When you see the conductor's beat, it has to register in your mind; you play, the organ has to speak, the resulting sound is heard by those you are accompanying—this whole process takes a certain amount of time. You must be aware of that, and (although it may only be a moment) allow for it. Never "drag", by being behind the beat with your playing. You must know and understand the instrument you are playing and how long it takes to speak, and you must estimate the resonance of the building.

Playing under a conductor imposes on the organist an

additional worry to his already full quota; he will consequently need to have the management of his instrument completely under control if he is to keep his attention on the beat and on the conductor's interpretation. On no account follow the school of second-rate organists who, after watching the first beat, go into hibernation until the last few bars when they glance at the conductor to see if there is a rallentando or not! Such is the height, or rather the depth, of amateurism in the bad sense of that word. You must be constantly susceptible to the musical ebb and flow, as well as mood and colour, which you can get from watching a good conductor.

The principles of variety, balance etc. which apply to accompaniment · are equally relevant to playing under a conductor. The conductor's job is to supply the tempo, the rhythm, to ensure accuracy, to bring out the musical effects, to listen for balance; so you must not take any criticism of such points, if they are directed towards you, the organist, as a personal insult. On the contrary, if the conductor makes his suggestions for improving the performance in any way, it means that he is interested enough to listen to the effect of the whole and that he wants to do his best to improve it. If he says for example, that the organ is too loud at any point, you would be well advised to accept his word for it. You may not have had the chance of hearing exactly the effect of the particular stops you were using from where he is standing. Do not whatever happens attempt to argue about it; the conductor is responsible for the result, and the organist must accept his decision. If you really feel very strongly, and have grounds for doing so, a private word afterwards would be perfectly reasonable.

If you have managed to practise the organ a good deal, and have taught yourself a certain amount of fluency in simple pieces, there is no reason why you should not be able to play satisfactorily under a conductor's beat. Provided he is a good conductor, you would benefit considerably and learn a number of points that no book can teach you. But there are three simple principles which apply particularly to this sort of accompaniment. As every organ is different it is impossible to particularise, but you must apply the general principles to your own particular case:

(1) Make sure that there is a good mirror in a convenient position (in front of you or at the side of the console) enabling you to see the conductor. With such a mirror, you will have no excuse for not watching the beat!

(2) Minimise stop changes as they will distract your attention from the beat. But beware, however, of letting your accompaniment become monotonous.

(3) If you are accompanying a choral performance let your accompaniment enhance and enrich the singing; do not impede it.

CHAPTER XIV

IMPROVISATION, TRANSPOSITION, SIGHT-READING

Importance of practical musicianship — Sense of form, time, key — Sequences — Contrapuntal devices — Design of a piece — Benefits derived — Knowledge of progressions needed for transpositions — Flat keys and sharp keys — Accidentals — Benefits of sight reading

> *Note*—In this chapter particularly, if the reader wishes to enquire further into the terms and expressions used, he is referred to the companion volumes in this series by King Palmer, "Teach Yourself to Compose music", "Teach Yourself Music".

(A) *Improvisation*

The growth of professionalism in the performance of music, which has been one of the most marked features of the last hundred years, naturally tended to push into the background the traditional art of improvisation (or playing spontaneously). Nowadays the performer, whatever his instrument, who includes an improvisation in his recital is a rarity indeed; partly because it is out of fashion to do so, partly (dare it be said?) because he has not the musicianship. For there is not the slightest doubt that to sit down and improvise intelligently requires musicianship of the highest order. Moreover, the complaint that "no one improvises nowadays" is by no means new; the great seventeenth-century organist Johann Reinken had the same idea, until one day, towards the end of his life, he heard Bach himself, then a young man of thirty-five, extemporise on a chorale, whereupon he changed his opinion.

The need and importance of improvisation is in exact proportion to your need to develop a practical musicianship at the keyboard. I do not, by "improvisation", mean filling up the few moments' hiatus in Mattins while the collecting plates are taken up at the end of the last hymn, (important though this is!) I mean training your musical imagination in such a way that it can produce impromptu a coherent, musical passage. All the greatest creative musicians have improvised; Bach did so for hours on end; Beethoven and Mozart each had the ability to pour out ideas onto the keyboard during a public recital; César Franck used to "think aloud" as it were, both on the piano and on the organ—his organ improvisations being held in the highest esteem; and the list could continue down to the present. Improvisation is often the way ideas are born.

Before suggesting some "dos", it is important to establish the more obvious "don'ts". The chief danger to guard against is shapelessness; playing without rhyme or reason, not knowing where you are. This is all too easy on the organ with its ready-made tone. An improvisation must be based on a definite sense of shape, it must give a feeling of design and structure. Next on the list of don'ts is the "one foot in the grave and the other on the Swell pedal" sort of playing. It is very easy to place your left foot firmly and immovably on a pedal note, leave it there, and proceed to play a succession of chords over it with the hands, the right foot meanwhile working overtime to produce "expression" with the Swell box! Needless to say, there is more in improvisation than this.

An improvisation must be based on a theme or subject, just as a composition is. If you are to improvise a short Prelude or Postlude, let it be formed round, or based on, a hymn-tune or other tune which you already have clearly fixed in your mind. If you are improvising your own subject, then let it be of a regular and definite formation, not vague and rambling. More of this in a moment. There is no reason why, if you have not had a chance to do a lot of improvisation hitherto, you should not jot down your main subject(s), and keep it in front of you on the console.

It is important to begin by improvising phrases that are short, simple, and of regular bar divisions; having done that successfully it is then possible to advance and work phrases that are longer and more complex. So let two bars be answered by two bars, four bars by four, and so on. Try to appreciate fully, and to understand why, if four bars are answered by three bars, the result is lop-sided. Here is a simple example of two symmetrical phrases, four bars answered by four bars, in the key of G major:

Imagine how "wrong" it would sound if I were to put the final cadence in bar 7 instead of bar 8.

Several fundamental points emerge from this simple beginning. There must be a definite sense of time and key. In this case 4/4, G major. Notice also that each of the two 4-bar phrases has a similar construction; that is to say 2 bars plus 2 bars; also that the first 2 bars in the second phrase correspond in rhythm with the first 2 bars of the first phrase. Notice also that the note values of each phrase are varied. This allows you to take any particularly interesting rhythmic pattern and develop it later on. If you do this, and the pattern is of sufficiently distinctive character, the listener will recognise that it belongs to the original subject. To improvise on a subject consisting of notes of the same value is a very much more difficult undertaking.

This example also contains a "half-close" on the Dominant in bar 4. See whether you can deduce the underlying harmony of the passage, as a knowledge of simple harmony and the fundamental progressions is clearly a matter of extreme importance. A good way of practising them is to play the principal cadences—Perfect, Imperfect, Plagal, Phrygian, Interrupted, Inverted—and aim to become fluent in them in as many different keys as you can. In any piece the need to have a scheme of keys, and key changes, is essential; you cannot remain in the key of the Tonic for a whole piece. That naturally means that you need to develop the ability to modulate from one key to another. One of the greatest helps to you in practising this is the ability to form "sequences"; in other words to take a phrase, or pattern of notes, and repeat it with the same basic formation but at a higher or lower pitch.

Suppose I wished to treat the opening 2 bars "sequentially", it might go:

If you introduce a cadence after a sequence you will find yourself in a different key from the original.

So before starting on your improvisation you must decide on the Time signature and the Key signature of the principal theme or subjects. Also the best speed, and its general character. In just the same way as an ordinary composition, give your improvisation a marking (in your mind's eye); e.g. Allegro vivace, Andante, Lento, etc. Is it to be played *p* or *f*? Try to realise, at the earliest possible moment, its potential source of interest, and bear that in mind as you play.

When harmonising a simple tune, always remember that one of the chief aims of a composer is to make his effect with the minimum number of notes. So keep your basic harmonies as simple as possible. Do not attempt to harmonise every note—think in bars rather than notes;

preferably, in this case, think in units of 2 bars, as that is how the subject is made up.

Certain things "go" on the organ; music of a contrapuntal nature is one of them. So remember to keep your improvisation as much as possible in parts, 2, 3, or 4, and to keep each part distinctive. Simple harmonisation with block chords, particularly thick chords, becomes tiresome after a while.

When you begin to work contrapuntally, there are several devices which may be of use in your improvised piece. The sequence mentioned above is only one. Others are the imitation of one part by another; inversion, which means turning the subject upside down; augmentation, or lengthening the value of notes; diminution, or shortening the value of notes; fugal treatment of the subject material; pedal points; changing the key from major to minor, minor to major; changing the time signature.

There is no need to keep the pedal part going continuously. Allow your feet a rest every now and then. And when they come in again, let them have a definite pedal entry (probably the principal subject), and not just a vague sound somewhere low down the pedal board. Often a staccato pedal is uncommonly effective, corresponding to the "pizzicato" of the Cellos and Basses in the orchestra.

It is as well to have a definite scheme for the various sections which make up your whole piece, and to train your mind to get used to regular bar-divisions, which will probably be a multiple of 4.

Such a scheme might be:

1st section   8 bars modulating to the Dominant
2nd section   8 bars modulating back to the Tonic

Or you might have a middle section separating these two, introducing entirely new material; that will have the advantage that when you bring back the principal subject in the last 8 bars it will sound fresh. It is always useful to remember that before starting the main subject you can with great effect have a short introduction of 2 bars or so—not too long, otherwise it will obscure the principal material—and similarly, at the end, a short Coda. What design you decide to have is really immaterial; but it is essential that you should have one.

The same principles of registration apply to improvisation as to any other piece. The stops used should be in keeping with the character of the piece. If it is possible for you to achieve a sense of growth or climax, then so much the better.

If you decide to improvise a Fugue—and why not?—you need particular care with the counter-subject; it must be both complementary to the main subject, yet distinctive in its own right, if it is to be of any use later on in the improvisation. If the main subject can be described as your thought, then the counter-subject may be described as your afterthought; much deeper! When you have brought in all the parts, or "voices", then introduce an "Episode" on the Swell, based on existing material. Vary it as much as possible by introducing some of the devices already suggested, and above all do not let the music degenerate into block chords. There is no reason why an Episode should not be in just two parts; even in a 4-part Fugue, there is no reason for all the parts to be speaking all the time! Then gradually bring your parts back onto the Great, where you should finish firmly. Improvising a Fugue is very much more difficult than a "straight" piece, and should only be attempted when you have first acquired a certain amount of fluency in the easier forms.

By practising improvisation you do two things. First you improve your fluency in playing and managing the organ, since you have no copy to claim your attention, and therefore your whole mind can be given to the playing itself. Secondly you improve immeasurably your knowledge and appreciation of finished compositions. You will find you sharpen your awareness of the sort of problems that a composer has to face and you will form a much sounder

judgment of the way he has solved them; thus you will be
better able to appreciate the music as a whole.

(B) *Transposition*

In order to play a passage in a different key from the one
in which it was written, you need to be thoroughly con-
versant with the normal progressions of Diatonic harmony,
and to know the degrees of the scale. As an example of what
I mean, if you see the following in a piece which is in
C major:

you should think of it not so much as a progression from the
chord of G to the chord of C, as a progression from the chord
of the Dominant (V) to the Tonic (I). Then in order to
transpose that progression you simply find the Dominant of
the new key and follow that by the Tonic, with the two
chords spaced to correspond to the original. You will at
once realise from this illustration of one of the commonest
progressions, that the most important part, and the one
which gives the clue to the whole passage, is the bass part.
It is invariably the bass part which determines the essential
nature of an ordinary chord; so start from the bottom and
work up!

The occasions on which you will be asked to transpose
will be extremely few and far between; but it is a good
exercise, and a test of whether you have really grasped a
piece. Hymns are the best possible means of beginning, so
long as you do not know them too thoroughly. Different
keys have a different character about them; and you may
find that a hymn tune written in the key of A♭ will sound a

very different thing from the same tune played in the key of A, although there is only a semitone difference in pitch between the two. Sometimes, indeed, this sort of "semitone" transposition does not count as transposition at all. If a piece is written in the key of A♭ major, in other words with four flats, and you wish to play it in the key of A major, which has three sharps, all that is needed is for you to use the same notation but pretend that the key-signature is three sharps instead of four flats. Pick up the first thing you find written in the key of A♭, and you will find this works perfectly. There are other "semitone" transpositions which can be done in the same way, by simply imagining a different key-signature.

Transposition becomes far more difficult, and much more of a worthwhile exercise, when the change is into a key a tone or more apart, or a semitone that requires a complete rethinking.

First decide whether the change is "up" or "down" in pitch. That only takes a few seconds. Next decide whether the change is "up" or "down" in terms of key. In other words is the new key higher and sharper than the old, or is it lower and flatter? The following diagram will help to show what I mean:

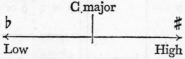

If a piece is written in the key of B♭ major (2 flats) and you are going to play it in the key of C major, you are going to transpose it "up" (in pitch) a tone. Moreover, the key of B♭ is a flat key, the key of C is neutral; so the change is up tonally speaking as well. But it is perfectly possible for a piece to be transposed "up" in pitch, and yet "down" tonally. For example if a piece is written in the key of G major (one sharp) and you change it into the key of A♭ major (four flats) you are transposing it "up" a semitone in pitch, yet tonally speaking "down", i.e. flatter.

E

Bear in mind continually what the new key-signature is, and in particular what notes are going to be affected by it, unless otherwise shown by accidentals. If a passage has no accidentals at all (extra sharps, flats, etc.), then to transpose it is a comparatively simple task, provided only that you think of the new key-signature, not the old one, and concentrate on the bass line.

But accidentals make transposition something of an obstacle race. The sign ♯ in the original key may, and probably will, imply a different sign in the new key. If you remember the fundamentals—that a ♯ raises a note by a semitone, a ♭ lowers it by a semitone; that a ♮ in a sharp key, if applied to a sharp in the key-signature lowers the note by a semitone, and in a flat key, in the same circumstances, raises the note by a semitone—if you remember that, then you will understand the purpose of the following table:

Table showing the treatment of accidentals in transposition

Original Accidental		Original key transposed	
		"up," to a sharper key	"down," to a flatter key
♭	becomes	♭ or ♮	♮ or ♭♭
♮	becomes	♮ or ♯	♮ or ♭
♯	becomes	♯ or x	♯ or ♮

An accidental may remain in its original form in the new key. This is so if it is placed before a note which is unaffected by either the old or the new key-signature. For example, if you transpose a passage from F major (one flat) to G major (one sharp), the following notes are unaffected by either the flat or the sharp:

$$G, \quad A, \quad C, \quad D, \quad E$$

G in the new key, the tonic, will correspond to F in the old key, both of these being "white" notes. Therefore F♯ in the original will simply become G♯ in the transposed version. The sharp remains a sharp. But B♭ in the original (the Subdominant, or 4th degree of the scale) corresponds to C in the new key. Therefore B♮ in the original will become C♯ in the transposed version. In this case the ♮, which raises the flattened note a semitone, becomes ♯. More examples of this sort of changing of accidentals will be found in the example given at the end of this section. The first thing to decide in your mind before starting to transpose is what effect the ♮ has in the original key, and what it is therefore likely to become in the new key.

Unfortunately for the transposer, several accidentals are not really accidentals at all, but are simply put in for the sake of academic exactitude, in order to counteract the implication of a ♯ or ♭ in the previous bar, or in another part. See whether you can detect any such "academic" accidentals in the exercise at the end of the section—there are six!

You may easily find yourself in awkward corners involving C♭ or Fx, but as I said at the outset you will manage transposition if you are acquainted with the commonest harmonic progressions, and are therefore able to anticipate where a part is likely to go. The greatest source of danger is likely to be the join between the end of one line and the beginning of the next, or at the turn of a page.

Finally let me say, do not do too much transposition; it is only a means to an end, that end being ability to play the organ. It can be useful in training your musical agility, particularly your knowledge of keys and key signatures, in much the same way as crossword puzzles sharpen one's agility with words. But a little goes a long way.

EXERCISE FOR TRANSPOSITION

Play a tone and semitone higher and lower.

F. J. R.

(C) *Sight-reading*

This is an important side of musicianship, which you would be very well advised to develop as much as you can; for there is no doubt that sight-reading can be developed, even if it cannot be learnt. Whether you are a successful sight-reader depends only on one thing, that is the speed and accuracy with which you can convert the printed score into sound. Can you, by simply looking at the copy, imagine to yourself the effect of its being played? This question leads directly to the best way by far of practising sight-reading, which is to follow a piece in the score—even one that you know thoroughly—while it is being played.

There is not a great deal that can usefully be said on this subject. It should go without saying that you must see and remember the key-signature and time-signature of the piece. The more you have the "feel" of the keyboard at your finger-tips, and are acquainted with intervals, the better. Above all keep the pulse both regular and continuous. Perhaps the best advice that can be given is that you should practise sight-reading, not read about it!

One of the greatest benefits of an ability to sight-read is that it enables you to make a preliminary study of a piece before deciding whether it deserves your closer attention. If you pick up a new and strange piece of music, and you are able to play it through so as to obtain a rough impression of it, then you can decide whether it is worth pursuing. The essential thing to remember is that you must play it continuously, even if what you play is only an approximation. It will be a nearer approximation than if you play in fits and starts, even possibly (in the latter case) playing more notes. It is better to omit some of the notes than to work them all out (or try to), and by so doing lose track of the basic movement of the piece. Do not aim for a finished performance straight away.

The pieces marked * at the end of Chapter XI are of an easier standard than the rest, and may well be within reach of your sight-reading ability. They may thus form a starting point for you. But the hymn-book will give you an excellent grounding in straightforward sight-reading, and if you have not had a lot of practice I strongly commend it to your notice.

Of these three aspects of an organist's musicianship, sight-reading is the most important. It is possible to survive musically without being able to improvise, though it goes without saying that you will be a better musician if you can.

And transposition is really only a gymnastic exercise; five minutes first thing in the morning will start the day right! But your ability to sight-read—in other words to look at a printed row of notes for the first time, and hear them as effective, musical sounds—is really the truest measure there is of your practical musicianship; if only because the more you are called on to play (and I hope you will be), the more you will require it.

IN CONCLUSION

THE organist shares with the pianist the great honour of being able to play a piece of music without any support from other musicians; he is essentially a soloist. Even when accompanying, or playing the Continuo part, he must be constantly aware that he controls under his fingers an instrument capable of the richest and most varied sounds of any.

Yet, although he is a soloist, his art is not commensurate with the art of music as a whole. As we have seen, the organ has several fundamental limitations—of rhythm, tone-colour, expression, and above all of repertoire. The successful organist must therefore understand and accept such limitations. Indeed only if he does that will his playing be convincing. As is often the case with human beings, this instrument of ours only reacts favourably to those who accept it as it is, not so much to those who wish or pretend that it were otherwise.

The number of foremost composers who have ignored the organ, or written only a handful of pieces for it out of their entire output, is too large for this to be entirely coincidental. The simplest and most reasonable explanation is that the organ has not seemed to them a satisfactory vehicle for their thoughts and ideas. The wisest course for the lover of the organ in such a situation is to treat it as inevitable rather than regrettable; and to enquire what were the thoughts and intentions of the great composers, and why the organ was not a suitable medium for them; and thus to come to some valid conclusion concerning what legitimate musical thoughts and moods the organ *can* effectively express.

Meanwhile there is enough fine music to occupy our attention, until some day (who knows?) the organ again comes into its own.

CLASSIFIED TABLE OF STOPS
MOST COMMONLY FOUND

Diapason (or Principal) stops

Contra Dulciana	16'
Contra Salicional	16'
Double Open Diapason	16'
Open metal	16'
Open wood	16'
Quintaton	16'
Dulciana	8'
Open Diapason	8', 16'
Salicional	8'
Voix Celeste	8'
Dulcet	4'
Octave	4'
Principal (Prestant)	4'
Salicet	4'
Fifteenth (Doublette)	2'
Superoctave	2'

Mixtures and Mutations

Acuta	
Carillon	
Cornet	
Cymbel	
Dulcet Twelfth	2⅔'
Echo Cornet	
Full mixture	
Furniture	
Mixture (Plein Jeu)	
Quint	10⅔', 5⅓', 2⅔'
Septieme	1⅐'
Sesquialtera	
Sharp mixture	
Tierce	1⅗'
Twelfth	2⅔'

String stops

Contra Geigen	16'
Contra Viola	16'
Violone	16'
Celeste	8', 16'
Gamba	8', 16'
Geigen	8', 4'
Geigen Principal	8'
Viola	8', 4'
Viola da Gamba	8'
Viole d'orchestre	8'
Violoncello	8'

Flute stops

Sub-Bourdon	32'
Sub-Bass	32'
Bourdon	16'
Contra-Bourdon	16'
Grosse Flote	16'
Sub-Bass	16'
Bass Flute	8'
Clarabel	8'
Cor de nuit	8'
Gedact (Gedackt)	8'
Hohlflöte	8'
Lieblich Gedact	8'
Quintadena	8'
Rohr Flute	8', 4'
Spitzflöte	8', 4'
Stopped Diapason	8'
Suabe Flute	8'
Flauto traverso	4'
Flute ouverte	4'
Gemshorn	4'
Harmonic Flute	4'

Stopped Flute	4'.	Fagotto (Bassoon)	16'
Waldflote	4'	Ophicleide	16'
Flageolet	2', 1'	Trombone (Posaune)	16'
Flautina	2'	Tuba	16', 8', 4'
Harmonic Piccolo	2'	Clarinet (Clarionet)	8'
Piccolo	2'	Cor Anglais	8'
Larigot	1⅓'	Cornopean	8'
Nazart (Nasard)	5⅓', 2⅔'	Cromorne (Krummhorn)	8'
		Horn	8'
Reed stops		Oboe	8'
Bombarde	16'	Orchestral Oboe	8'
Contra Fagotto	16'	Posaune	8'
Contra Posaune	16'	Tromba	8'
Contra Tromba	16'	Trumpet (Trompette)	8'
Double Clarinet	16'	Vox Humana	8'
Double Oboe	16'	Clarion (Clairon)	4'
Double Trumpet	16'	Schalmei	4'

E*

SPECIFICATIONS OF
CERTAIN SELECTED ORGANS

Bach's organ at St. Thomas, Leipzig.

Great

(1)	Principal	16'
(2)	Principal	8'
(3)	Quintaton	16'
(4)	Octave	4'
(5)	Quinte	3'
(6)	Superoctave	2'
(7)	Spielpfiefe	8'*
(8)	Sesquialtera	
(9)	Mixtur (6, 8 & 10 ranks)	

Swell

(1)	Grobgedackt	8'
(2)	Principal	4'
(3)	Nachthorn	4'
(4)	Nasat	3'
(5)	Gemshorn	2'
(6)	Cymbel (2 ranks)	
(7)	Sesquialtera	
(8)	Regal	8'
(9)	Geigen Regal	8'

Choir

(1)	Principal	8'
(2)	Quintaton	8'
(3)	Lieblich Gedackt	8'
(4)	Kleingedackt	4'
(5)	Querflote	4'
(6)	Violine	2'
(7)	Rauschquinte doppelt	
(8)	Mixtur (4 ranks)	
(9)	Sesquialtera	
(10)	Spitzflote	4'
(11)	Schallflote	1'
(12)	Krummhorn	8'
(13)	Trompete	8'

Pedal

(1)	Subbass (metal)	16'
(2)	Posaune	16'
(3)	Trompete	8'
(4)	Schalmei	4'
(5)	Cornet	. 2'

Notice particularly the Pedal Organ, with its comprehensive Reed chorus, and its single flue stop. The Mixture work throughout is highly developed.

* A flute-quality stop.

César Franck's organ at St. Clotilde, Paris.
(Cavaille–Coll)

Recit (III)

Quintaton	16'
Bourdon	8'
Flute Harmonique	8'
Gambe	8'
Voix Celeste	8'
Voix Humaine	8'
Hautbois	8'
Flute	4'
Clarinette	8'
Nasard	2⅔'
Octavin	2'
Tierce	1⅗'
Plein Jeu	4 ranks
Bombarde	16'
Trompette	8'
Clairon	4'

Positif (II)

Bourdon	16'
Bourdon	8'
Flute Harmonique	8'
Gambe	8'
Montre	8'
Salicional	8'
Prestant	4'
Flute	4'
Quinte	2⅔'
Doublette	2'
Tierce	1⅗'
Plein Jeu	4 ranks
Piccolo	1'

Trompette	8'
Clairon	4'

Grand Orgue (I)

Montre	16'
Bourdon	16'
Bourdon	8'
Flute Harmonique	8'
Gambe	8'
Montre	8'
Prestant	4'
Flute	4'
Quinte	2⅔'
Doublette	2'
Cornet	
Plein Jeu	7 ranks
Bombarde	16'
Trompette	8'
Clairon	4'

Pedale

Soubasse	32'
Contre Basse	16'
Bourdon	16'
Flute	8'
Flute	4'
Doublette	2'
Basson	16'
Bombarde	16'
Trompette	8'
Clairon	4'

Note: Only a few stops have been added since César Franck's day.

The organe at the Odeon Cinema, Marble Arch, London.
(Christie)

Pedal		*Couplers*	

(Chamber A)

Solo

Phonon Bass	16′		
Tibia clausa	16′	**(Chamber A)**	
Bourdon	16′	Contra Tibia clausa	16′
Contra viola	16′	Trombone	16′
Ophicleide	16′	Vox humana	16′
Tuba horn	16′	Tibia clausa	8′
Saxophone	16′	Fanfare trumpet	8′
Stop quint	10⅔′	Saxophone	8′
Tibia clausa	8′	Vox humana	8′
Viola	8′	Tibia clausa	4′
Bass flute	8′	Vox humana	4′
Tuba horn	8′	Cathedral chimes	
Saxophone	8′	Muted chimes	
Flute major	4′		
Flute minor	4′		

(Chamber B)

Diaphone horn	32′		
Violone	16′	**(Chamber B)**	
Contra salicional	16′	Contra tuba sonora	16′
Bassoon	16′	Bass clarinet	16′
Clarinet	16′	Orchestral flute	8′
Clarinet	8′	Quintadena	8′
Violoncello	8′	Synthetic cello	8′
Salicional	8′	Tuba sonora	8′
Synthetic cello	8′	Clarinet	8′
Piano	16′	Orchestral oboe	8′
Piano	8′	Musette	8′
Bass drum tap (soft		Orchestral piccolo	2′
Tom-Tom		Piano	8′
		Harp	8′

Second Touch

Tibia clausa	16′	Celesta	4′
Tuba horn	8′	Tubular chimes	
Bass drum tap (loud)		Glockenspiel	
Bass drum roll		Orchestral bells	
Crash Cymbals		Vibraphone	
Cymbal roll		Xylophone	
Cathedral chimes		Sleigh bells	
Muted chimes		Triangle	
		Cymbal choke tap	

Accompaniment		*Great*	
(Chamber A)		(Chamber A)	
Bourdon	16'	Contra Tibia clausa	16'
Contra viole d'amour	16'	Bourdon	16'
Strings	16'	Contra viola	16'
Open diapason	8'	Tuba horn	16'
Tibia clausa	8'	Saxophone	16'
Gedackt	8'	Diapason phonon	8'
Hohl flote	8'	Open diapason	8'
Viole d'orchestre	8'	Tibia clausa	8'
Strings	8'	Gedackt	8'
Viole d'amour	8'	Viola	8'
Tuba horn	8'	Viole d'orchestre	8'
Saxophone	8'	Strings	8'
Vox humana	8'	Tuba horn	8'
Stopped flute	4'	Fanfare trumpet	8'
Hohl flute	4'	Saxophone	8'
Strings	4'	Stopped quint	5⅓'
Octave viole d'amour	4'	Octave diapason	4'
Stopped twelfth	2⅔'	Tibia clausa	4'
Piccolo	2'	Stopped flute	4'
Flute mixture		Viola	4'
Piano	8'	Strings	4'
Harp	8'	Tuba horn	4'
Celesta	4'	Tibia twelfth	2⅔'
Snare drum tap		Octave viole	4'
Snare drum roll		Piccolo	2'
Tom-Tom		Stopped twelfth	2⅔'
Wood block tap		Tierce	1⅗'
Tambourine		Brilliant mixture	
Castanets		Piano	16'
Jingles		Piano	8'
Sand block		Piano	4'

Second Touch			
Diapason phenon	8'		
Tuba horn	8'		
Cathedral chimes		Second Touch	
Triangle		Fanfare trumpet	8'
Cymbal tap		Cathedral chimes	
Muted chimes		Glockenspiel	
Snare drum roll		Snare drum roll	
Wood block roll		Muted chimes	

Couplers

Orchestral
(Chamber B)

Violone	16′
Muted strings	16′
Contra salicional	16′
Gemshorn diapason	8′
Violoncello	8′
Violins	8′
Muted strings	8′
Salicional	8′
Salicional quint	5⅓′
Octave violoncello	4′
Violins	4′
Muted strings	4′
Salicet	4′
Salicet twelfth	2⅔′
Salicetina	2′
Echo mixture	
Cornet de violes	
Quintadena	8′
Contra tibia minor	16′
Bassoon	16′
Tibia minor	8′
Oboe horn	8′
Clarinet	8′
Orchestral oboe	8′
Tuba sonora	8′

(Chamber B)—*cont.*

Tibia minor	4′
Flageolet	2′
Contra trumpet	16′
Trumpet	8′
Clarion	4′
Snare drum tap	
Snare drum roll	
Tom-Tom	
Wood block tap	
Tambourine	
Castanets	
Jingles	
Sand block	

Second Touch

Vibraphone
Xylophone
Sleigh bells
Triangle
Cymbal tap
Tubular chimes
Snare drum roll
Wood block roll

Accessories include:
  2 balanced swell pedals
  10 Tremulants

APPENDIX 3

GLOSSARY OF TERMS COMMONLY FOUND IN ORGAN MUSIC

(F) = French word
(G) = German word
(I) = Italian word

A

Accouplez (F)	Couple
Acoustic Bass	Pedal stop of 32′
Affettuoso (I)	Affectionate
Affretare (I)	To hurry
Ajoutez (F)	Add
Anche (F)	Reed
Animé (F), Animato (I)	Animated, lively
Ausdruck (G)	Feeling
Ausdrucksvoll (G)	With feeling (= Espressivo)
Ausgabe (G)	Edition

B

Bearbeitet (G)	Arranged
Bereite vor (G)	Prepare (i.e. stops)
Bewegt (G)	Movement
Bewegter (G)	Move faster (= piu mosso)
Boite fermee (F)	Swell box shut
Boite ouverte (F)	Swell box open
Bombarde	(a) Powerful 16′ reed
	(b) Manual containing powerful reed stops
Brustwerk (G)	Choir organ

C

Canzona	A simple, short composition
Cedez (F)	Give way, i.e. get slower (= rall)
Chorale Prelude	A composition formed round a Chorale, or Hymn-tune

Chorus	A combination of stops, usually of the same family, but of different pitch (e.g. Reeds 16', 8' and 4')
Cipher	The continuous sounding of a note due to some defect in the mechanism
Clavier (F)	Keyboard
Composition Pedals	Pedals controlling groups of stops
Concave	Referring to the Pedal-board of an organ, this indicates that the pedals dip slightly towards the centre, and are not perfectly flat from one side to the other.
Continuo (or "Basso Continuo", or "Thorough Bass")	As its name implies, a continuous part, played on the organ or harpsichord, which provides the "stuffing" for an orchestra; used in early music, particularly of the Bach–Handel period. The player may find he has to deduce the necessary harmonies as he plays, and work out a "figured bass".
Coupler	A stop or other device for joining two manuals, or pedals and manual, together.

D

Dehors, en dehors (F)	Brought out, i.e. as a solo
Desaccouplez (F)	Uncouple
Doch (G)	Yet
Dolce (I)	Sweet
Doppel (G)	Double
Dunkel (G)	Dark (e.g. referring to 16' stops)

E

Echoklavier (G)	Choir organ (cf. Unterwerk)
Elargissant (F)	Broadening (= allargando)
Enlevez (F)	Push in, i.e. stop using
Etwas (G)	Somewhat

F

Fach (G)	Times. This word is used to indicate the number of ranks in a mixture stop (e.g. Mixtur 4 fach)

Fermata (I)	Pause. (written ⌒)
Fermez (F)	Shut
Figured Bass	A single line of notes in the Bass clef, making up the Bass part. Under the notes are numbers corresponding to the type of chord required. e.g.

6 = First inversion
$\frac{6}{4}$ = Second inversion
5 = Common chord

Other numbers (2, 7) indicate that the chord contains these intervals

Flue	That type of pipe in which tone is produced by air vibrating in the pipe.
Fonds (F)	"Foundation" stops; stops fundamental to the organ. This means every stop except Reeds, mutations and mixtures, which are collectively called "jeux de combinaison"
Frei (G)	Free
Full	All available stops

G

Grand Choeur (F)	(a) Full organ
	(b) Manual containing powerful, brilliant stops
Grand Orgue	(a) Great Organ (i.e. the Great manual) Sometimes written G
	(b) The main, largest organ in the west-end of a church. The smaller (Choir) organ would be used for accompaniment only.
Grob (G)	Coarse, rough

H

H (G)	B flat
Hauptwerk (G)	Great organ

I

Immer (G)	Always (= sempre)
Innig (G)	With feeling

J

Jeu (F)	Stop
Jeux doux (F)	Soft stops

L

Laisser (F)	Leave
Langsam (G)	Slow
Largement (F), Largamente (I)	Broadly
Lebhaft (G)	Lively
Leicht (G)	Light

M

Maggiore (I)	Major
Main droite, M.D. (F)	Right hand
Main gauche, M.G. (F)	Left hand
Massig (G)	In moderate time (= moderato)
Meno (I)	Less
Mettez (F)	Draw (a stop), i.e. bring into use
Modere (F)	In moderate time (= moderato)
Moll (G)	Minor
Montre (F)	Open Diapason pipe, so called because it is in front of the instrument, and therefore easily seen

N

Nach und nach (G)	Gradually
Nicht (G)	Not
Noch (G)	Still more

O

Oberwerk (G)	Swell organ
Ohne (G)	Without
Organo di Coro (I)	Choir organ
Organo d'espressione (I)	Swell organ
Orgel (G)	Organ
Orgelwerke (G)	Compositions for organ
Otez (F)	Push in, i.e. stop using
Ouvrez (F)	Open

P

Partitur (G), Partition (F)	Score
Passacaglia	Composition built on a repeated Bass line, in triple time
Peu a peu (F)	Gradually (= poco a poco)
Pied (F)	Foot
Pitch	The height or depth of a note. A stop can be given 16′ or 4′ pitch, or any other, according to the length of the pipe
Plein Jeu	(a) Mixture stop (b) Full organ, without reeds (cf. Great to Mixture)
Portative	An early type of movable organ, such as the Regal
Positif (F)	Choir organ
Positive	An early type of organ that could not be moved
Prestant	Diapason of 4′ pitch
Principal	(a) The main stop, i.e. the Diapason (b) The 4′ Diapason
Principale (I)	Great organ

R

Radiating (pedals)	The pedals turned slightly outwards, not absolutely parallel
Rank	A set of pipes
Récit (F)	Swell organ, sometimes written R
Reed	A pipe in which the tone is produced by a vibrating tongue
Regal	An early portable organ
Retenu (F), Ritenuto (I)	Held back, slower
Retirez (F)	Push in (a stop)
Ricercar	A composition in fugal style, involving contrapuntal and canonic complications
Rohrwerk (G)	Reeds
Ruckpositif (G)	A small Choir organ, situated behind the player
Ruhig (G)	Peaceful

S

Sanft (G)	Soft
Sans (F)	Without
Scale	When referring to pipes, this word means the diameter
Schnell (G)	Quick
Schwellwerk (G)	Swell organ
Sehr (G)	Very
Serre (F)	Quicker
Stark (G)	Strong, firm
Stimme (G)	A stop

T

Tendre (F)	Tender
Tirasse (F)	Pedal Coupler e.g. Tirasse du Récit = Swell to Pedal
Touch	The process of pressing down, holding and releasing a key, whether manual or pedal
Tutti (I)	Full
Tuyaux (F)	Pipes

U

Unterwerk (G)	Choir organ (cf. Echoklavier)

V

Ventil pedal	A pedal which brings into action stops previously drawn, by letting wind into the appropriate wind chest. It is found on French organs
Vif (F)	Lively
Vorbereiten (G)	Prepare

Z

Zu (G)	Too
Zugehend (G)	Going
Zunge (G)	Reed

APPENDIX 4

SELECT BIBLIOGRAPHY

A   Technical books on organ building

The Organ, W. L. Sumner (Macdonald). (A most comprehensive book.)

The Electric Organ, Reginald Whitworth.

A Student's guide to the Organ, Reginald Whitworth (Musical Opinion).

The Organ—its tonal structure and registration, Cecil Clutton and George Dixon (Grenville Publishing Co.).

The Electronic Musical Instrument Manual, Alan Douglas (Pitman).

Electronic Organs, Robert L. Eby (Van Kampen Press–Musical Opinion).

B   Books and Primers on organ playing

Method for the Organ, Marcel Dupre (Leduc–United Music Publishers).

Method for the organ, Fernando Germani (De Santis–Rome).

Ars Organi, Flor Peeters (Hinrichsen).

Modern Organ pedalling, C. H. Phillips (Oxford University Press).

Systematic Organ pedal technique, R. Goss Custard (Stainer and Bell).

Exercises for organists (2 sets), C. S. Lang (Novello).

Improvisation on the organ, Hennie Schonten (W. Paxton & Co.).

C   Acoustics, general musical principles

The Nature of Music, Hermann Scherchen (Dobson).

Science and Music, Sir James Jeans (Cambridge University Press).

The Interpretation of Music, Thurston Dart (Hutchinson). (Particularly applicable to early music.)

D   Suggested books on individual composers, general history

J. S. Bach (2 volumes), Albert Schweitzer (A. and C. Black).

Two centuries of Bach, Frederick Blume (Oxford University
Press).

Keyboard music from the Middle Ages to the Baroque, G. S.
Bedbrook (Macmillan). (This contains an excellent bibliography for early organs and organ music.)

The complete organist, Harvey Grace (Richards Press).

The History of Music, Cecil Gray (Kegan Paul).

Music in England, Eric Blom (Penguin Books).

The Oxford Companion to Music, Percy Scholes (Oxford.
University Press).

César Franck, Leon Vallas (Harrap).

La musique d'orgue Francaise, N. Dufourcq (Floury–Paris).

E   Periodicals dealing with the organ

The Organ	Quarterly
The Musical Times	Monthly
Musical Opinion	Monthly

NOTE ON THE MIXTURE STOP

THE Mixture stop stands in isolation from other stops, both by reason of its unusual tone-colour, and its basic conception. The technicalities of its construction are more involved than in the case of other stops, and its use is equally hedged about with special considerations.

It is today a basic principle of acoustics that any note which sounds consists of a "Fundamental" and its "Overtones". That is to say the vibrations (whether of air or of a string or whatever) which cause a note to sound also bring into play subsidiary vibrations which in turn sound the "harmonics" of the original note. The "Fundamental" is the strongest; the overtones are less audible, but can be detected by a sensitive ear. (There are said to be 1024 altogether, which can be detected!) These overtones (or "Harmonics", or "Upper Partials") are together called the notes of the Harmonic Series. If low C is the Fundamental note struck, the notes of the Harmonic series would be:

You will see at a glance that the strongest Harmonics are the Octave and the Twelfth (i.e. the 2nd and 3rd harmonics); next come the Fifteenth and Seventeenth from the Fundamental (i.e. the 4th and 5th Harmonics). The Mixture sounds these basic intervals above the note pressed down, the number of Harmonics obviously depending on the number of Ranks the stop possesses.

There is an important corollary to this. Just as a Fundamental can suggest its attendant Harmonics, so two notes sounding together the 2nd and 3rd Harmonics can suggest the Fundamental. The "Acoustic Bass" stop works on this principle, to give 32′ tone. This principle also applies to the Mixture stop of some early organs.

But the interesting point is this. The Mixture stop has existed since the very earliest organs. Why? In comparison with the ancient craft of organ building, the science of Acoustics is a recent invention; words like "Harmonic series" or "Fundamental" had not been invented when the earliest organ builders were at work. Therefore to say that they made their mixture stops to conform with the notes of the Harmonic series is an anachronism. The only reasonable answer is that they made their Mixture stops simply because their musical instinct and judgment told them there was a need for such a stop, and because they liked the sound produced. As it happened they were completely right in their choice of "Harmonics"; the discoveries of Sauveur and Rameau have completely vindicated their work.

It is perhaps misleading to look at the specification of an early organ, and to shudder at what you imagine the Mixture work would sound like. But it is true to say that the less scientific theory there is available, and the less mass production there is of organ parts, the more the musical judgment of the organ builder is taxed, the more he must experiment by trial and error. He cannot sit down and calculate what the result ought to be theoretically; he has to go and listen. There is no reason to suppose that sixteenth- and seventeenth-century organ builders were not constantly experimenting with (among others) the mixture stop in order to find the best result. The highly developed state that the organ had reached by 1700 strongly suggests immense research and listening. As it happens, stops which appear on paper simply as mixture stops often produce a deep, rich tone, for the reason mentioned above.

As we have discussed elsewhere, one of the limitations of the organ is that it cannot, as an orchestra can, bring together blocks of contrasting tone quality to give a "tutti" effect; but all its parts are of the same tone quality. Its characteristic build-up comes from its depth and range of tone, of which the Mixture stop is an essential ingredient, and has been since organs began.

I have seen fit to mention this since there is a considerable "anti-Mixture" feeling among many who listen to and appreciate organ music. It is true that some organs with high wind-pressure have the shrillest and most penetrating Mixtures, which even full flues and reeds cannot support, and against which any sensitive ear would rebel. But it is unreasonable to generalize from such individual cases.

To say, as some do if further pressed, that the Mixture stop is "unmusical" is just not true. It has its origin in the musical instinct and judgment of organ builders over the centuries, which have since been completely vindicated by scientific research. On the contrary, the Mixture stop properly used is without rival for giving the organ additional brilliance and range of tone-colour.

INDEX